Absence

An Examination of the Thelma Young Murder Case

Lynne Blanchard

Copyright © 2016 by Lynne Blanchard.

All rights reserved. No part of this publication may be reproduced, distributed or transmitted in any form or by any means, including photocopying, recording, or other electronic or mechanical methods, without the prior written permission of the publisher, except in the case of brief quotations embodied in critical reviews and certain other noncommercial uses permitted by copyright law.

Book Layout ©2016 BookDesignTemplates.com

ISBN 978-1537480824

Absence of Evidence/Lynne Blanchard.

Preface

In 2006, the brutal murder of Michelle Young made national headlines. Michelle lived with her husband, Jason and two year old daughter Cassidy in a quiet Raleigh suburb. The couple was expecting a baby boy in four months. How could anyone harm a young pregnant mother? What happened to Michelle? Was there justice for Michelle?

I began researching questionable cases after following a murder trial in my county in 2011. I discovered that things aren't always as they appear. Sometimes the evidence doesn't support the prosecution's claims and the result is devastating—the conviction of an innocent person. It also means that the perpetrator(s) remain free to kill again. There is much doubt about the outcome of the Young case. This book will walk you through the Youngs' lives preceding the murder and the ensuing murder investigation and legal proceedings. In particular you will learn the truth about the "right" to remain silent. Silence *can* be used against you.

I would like to acknowledge my husband, Tim for his amazing support as I spent many hours researching this case. I would also like to thank Dr. Maurice Godwin for sharing valuable documents and photos from his work on this case. I am also very grateful to the Young family for helping me gain an understanding of this case from their perspective.

Contents

Contents

Introduction 1

Jason and Michelle 27

Coping with the news 33

Crime scene observations 51

Alibis 61

Neighborhood witnesses 65

Jason's relationships 69

2007 75

Convenience store witness 87

Was the crime scene staged? 95

Timeline and phone calls 103

Surveillance camera shenanigans 109

2008 115

2009 131

Trial 135

Jason is released 163

A new suspect? 165

Trial two 175

Appeal 189

Author's thoughts 197

CHAPTER 1

Introduction

Lives were forever shattered on November 3, 2006 when Michelle Young was found dead on the floor of the master bedroom. It was clear she had suffered a brutal slaying. Thankfully, her two year old daughter, Cassidy was left unharmed. Who was responsible for this heinous crime? What would investigators uncover?

***

Michelle lived with her husband, Jason and daughter, Cassidy in a quiet suburb of Raleigh, North Carolina. Their spacious brick home in the Enchanted Oaks community provided everything they needed—a fenced yard with a nice play-set for Cassidy, plenty of room for their dog to run, and lots of space for entertaining—which they loved to do. The home sat far back from the road. Brick pillars with lamps illuminated the driveway entrance, which was very dark at night.

Jason, thirty-two, and Michelle, twenty-nine, had just celebrated their third wedding anniversary on October 10. They had good jobs, a healthy daughter and had recently learned that Michelle was expecting a boy. Though the couple conceived unexpectedly with the first baby—prompting a wedding sooner than either had anticipated, this baby was planned, and they would finally be able to choose a name, shop for baby clothes and decorate the nursery. As an added bonus, a son would carry on the family name. However, the excitement over the new addition was somewhat overshadowed by ongoing issues within the relationship.

Jason and Michelle had occasional arguments over mundane things, such as chores and responsibilities. Their personalities differed—Michelle was very organized and Jason tended to procrastinate, so sometimes conflicts arose. There was also tension over their sex life. Jason was dissatisfied with what he characterized as a lack of sex in the marriage. This issue was no secret, as Jason complained about it to others and so did Michelle, though more discreetly. Michelle admitted that she had intimacy issues and Jason encouraged her to seek counseling to overcome them. Michelle did so in the weeks prior to her death.

Probably the largest source of discord in the marriage was Michelle's mother, Linda Fisher, particularly in the latter part of that year. Michelle's frequent calls to Linda about their arguments put an added strain on the marriage. Jason didn't appreciate Michelle speaking negatively about him to her family and he felt that Linda was unfairly judgmental of him when he rarely had an opportunity to share his side of the story.

Linda had a big influence on the relationship and convinced Michelle that her husband should be treating her better. For example, Linda was vocal about Jason's failure to buy Michelle a gift for their anniversary. He had been out of town on their anniversary but mailed her a hand-written card with Starbuck's gift cards inside. Linda expressed disappointment that he hadn't done more for her daughter. Jason was frustrated with his mother-in-law's meddling as he realized that it had a negative effect on their marriage, but the couple was trying to work through their conflicts.

Michelle's younger sister, Meredith offered to act as a mediator for the couple and they decided to take her up on the offer. The sisters grew up in Sayville, New York with their parents, Alan and Linda Fisher. Michelle moved to Raleigh in 1996 to attend North Carolina State University and had lived there ever since. Meredith moved in with Michelle and Jason when Cassidy was born in March 2004 because the couple needed a nanny and Meredith needed a fresh start. The sisters had never really gotten along, but Cassidy's birth seemed to draw them closer together.

Meredith resided with the Young family for a few months, and once she became familiar with the area she found her own apartment but continued to care for Cassidy while the Youngs were at work. She became quite attached to Cassidy from the very beginning and loved spending time with her, as aunts typically do.

In early 2006 Linda purchased a home in the Raleigh suburb of Fuquay-Varina. The thought was that Meredith could live there for now and she would have a home in the area when she retired later that year. She looked forward to moving to the Raleigh area to be near her daughters and grandchildren. The Fuquay home was just a short fifteen minute drive from Jason's and Michelle's Birchleaf home. Meredith and her best friend Colleen (also from New York) settled into the home.

For the time being, Linda remained in New York where she worked as a teacher, but she visited Raleigh as often as she could. Having the summers off, she liked to spend a bulk of that time in Raleigh. Oddly, she never stayed with Meredith in the brand new Fuquay home she had recently purchased. She always stayed with Jason and Michelle. Jason was beginning to get annoyed with her frequent and sometimes lengthy visits. It was too much. After Linda visited the couple for ten days in October 2006, Jason told Michelle that the length of her future visits would have to be limited to three to four days. Though Jason felt it was a reasonable compromise; Michelle disagreed. She loved having her mother around to help. The couple was struggling to resolve this particular conflict.

Linda bought Disney tickets for everyone—Jason, Michelle, Cassidy, Linda and Meredith were all booked for the trip to Orlando, which was to occur the third week of November. Thanksgiving would follow and Jason looked forward to taking Michelle and Cassidy to Brevard to spend the holiday with his family. Jason's mother, Pat and step-father, Gerald lived in Brevard, where Jason was raised. Brevard was in the mountains of North Carolina, about a four hour drive from Raleigh.

Linda wanted to tag along on the trip, but Jason was opposed to that. After all, they would have just completed the Florida trip. It was too much mother-in-law time. He wanted to enjoy the holiday with *his* family. Plus Christmas wasn't far off and Linda would be visiting again for at least a few days, if not more.

Michelle couldn't understand why Jason wouldn't want her mother to come along for the trip, and it resulted in a contentious argument.

To make matters worse, with the new baby coming, Michelle wanted her mother to move in with them—at least temporarily. She thought Linda could stay in an unfinished room in the attic. Linda even offered to pay to have an additional bathroom installed and finish off the space so she would have a comfortable place to stay. Plus the present guest-room would soon become a nursery for the new baby—all the more reason to convert the attic space to an additional bedroom. Jason was opposed to the idea. He wanted to finish the attic space, but not for his mother-in-law.

Linda's plan was to purchase a beach house, which would be just a two to three hour drive from Raleigh. She wanted to commute back and forth and spend three nights at the Birchleaf home each week and when the grandchildren got older, she could take them to the beach house with her for a few days on occasion. Michelle even drafted up a proposal to begin working part-time Tuesdays through Thursdays to coincide with Linda being there to watch the children.

Jason certainly wasn't agreeable to Linda moving in—even on a temporary basis, but Michelle had difficulty understanding his position. She was grateful for her mother's offer to help with the childcare and couldn't understand why Jason refused it. In fact, Jason didn't understand why Linda would need to stay with them *at all* once she moved to North Carolina. After all, she had the Fuquay home. Why couldn't she stay with Meredith?

Jason and Michelle recognized that they needed outside help to address the ongoing conflict about how often Linda should be around. For the time being, they were hoping Meredith would be able to help them sort through these issues. Clearly they weren't getting anywhere on their own. Jason believed Meredith was level-headed and that she could understand his viewpoints. He wanted things to get better. He wanted to find a way to minimize Linda's influence on his marriage. Michelle wanted to find a way to convince Jason that it was a good idea to have Linda around more to help out. They would have to come to some sort of compromise.

Not long after Linda's October visit, Jason decided to surprise Michelle with a belated anniversary gift. He thought a really nice leather purse would make the perfect gift since leather was the traditional three year anniversary gift. Jason and Michelle went out to dinner to celebrate their anniversary while Linda was in town to baby-sit Cassidy, but unfortunately they got into an argument that night. Jason wanted to make it up to Michelle and he hoped the gift would also put him in Linda's good graces since he knew she was unhappy that he hadn't done more for their anniversary. He discussed the gift idea with Meredith and she agreed that Michelle would like it. Meredith even offered to help him choose one for her, and Jason was grateful for the offer.

Thursday November 2, 2006

Michelle spent a typical day at Progress Energy where she worked as a financial analyst. She was anxious to present her manager with the proposal soon that would allow her to work part-time when the new baby arrived. She spent a lot of time outlining the specifics and included specific details about how the reduced hours would look. The baby wasn't due for four more months, but Michelle was very organized and wanted to have everything worked out well in advance of the baby's birth.

Michelle picked Cassidy up from daycare and arrived home at around five o'clock. She was looking forward to seeing her friend Shelly that evening. Shelly was going to grab some Italian take-out food and they would have dinner, catch up, and then watch Grey's Anatomy. The two had been friends since college where they were sorority sisters at NC State. They ended up sharing a condo together for a few years until Michelle got married. Despite their busy lives, they still managed to find the time to see each other. This particular get-together was planned because both of their husbands traveled a lot. Since Jason had travel plans that evening, they decided it would be a good opportunity for them to get together. Shelly had recently returned from her honeymoon and wanted to share some photos with Michelle.

Jason worked from home that day, and then mowed the lawn, did some yard work and hung up a hammock. He wanted the yard to look especially nice since his father-in-law, Alan Fisher was planning to visit from New Jersey that coming weekend. Jason got along great with Alan and was looking forward to seeing him. Michelle and Jason would also be tailgating for a NC State football game on Saturday. Alan would possibly babysit Cassidy if it was too cold to take her to the game. Tailgating was something the Youngs had enjoyed since college and they held lifetime season tickets since both had graduated from NC State. They would always meet up with a large group of friends and enjoyed hanging out before the games.

When the yard work was finished, Jason spent a little time researching purse options for Michelle's gift. He found a few Coach purses he thought Michelle might like on eBay, so he printed some images to show Meredith. He also printed directions to Clintwood, Virginia—the location of his first sales call Friday morning. By that time, Shelly had arrived with the food. She offered some to Jason, but he said he was looking forward to eating at a Cracker Barrel on his way to Virginia. He planned to break up the drive and stop at a hotel when he started feeling tired. This would leave him with just a short drive to Clintwood in the morning.

Michelle and Shelly gave Cassidy her bath, and then dressed her in a long-sleeve pink undershirt, a matching set of printed pink fleece pajamas, and white socks. The heat pump wasn't working upstairs and Michelle wanted to ensure that Cassidy would be warm enough. Jason kissed Michelle and Cassidy goodbye and left the house at around seven o'clock. He stopped at a gas station near home to fill up for the trip. While there he talked to his mom, Pat and told her that he was thinking about stopping by the next afternoon so he could visit for a bit and pick up some furniture that he wanted to put in the attic room. Jason figured that since he would already be so far west, it wouldn't be too out of the way for him to make his way south following his sales appointments, and maybe he would even spend Friday night at his mom's Brevard home, and then head home Saturday in time for the football game. His plans were tentative because he was still waiting for confirmation that Alan was coming to visit. If Alan was coming, he would not spend the night at his mom's. He would call Michelle later to find out for sure.

Jason was close to his mom and they ended up talking for close to an hour. She loved hearing about Cassidy and the plans for the new baby.

Jason headed west on Interstate 40 and would eventually head northwest toward Wytheville, Virginia. The route is difficult because there is always very heavy traffic through Greensboro. After getting through Greensboro, there are small highways that lead to Interstate 77 and the winding, mountainous roads require intense focus making for an arduous drive.

Michelle put Cassidy to bed and they were just about to begin watching Grey's Anatomy when Cassidy wandered downstairs with her pajama pants missing, diaper removed. She would typically remove her pants and wet diaper and walk around like that until one of her parents dressed her. Shelly tried to put a fresh diaper on Cassidy, but she insisted that her mom had to do it.

Soon after Michelle put Cassidy back to bed, Michelle's father, Alan called and told her he would not be able to make it that weekend. He had recently received a cancer diagnosis and wasn't up for the trip to North Carolina. Michelle was very disappointed and didn't understand why he wouldn't make the trip, despite his health concerns.

Meredith also phoned to ask if she would be needed to babysit on Saturday. She worked as a waitress and manager at Lucky 32 restaurant and wanted to know how to schedule her shifts for the next couple of days. The call was very brief; in fact Michelle never informed Meredith that Shelly was there and Shelly had no idea that Meredith had called.

Shelly noted how dark it was that night. The windows didn't have any blinds and she felt uneasy. She would later recall that she felt like they were being watched. She asked Michelle if she ever got scared being alone in the house and Michelle said "If someone wants to get in the house, they will."

> Mrs. Schaad was asked if Mrs. Young was a safety-type person. Mrs. Schaad stated she felt she was. Mrs. Schaad was asked if the house appeared to be secured to her. Mrs. Schaad stated that the inside of the home did not have any curtains/blinds and it "freaked" her out. Mrs. Schaad was asked to explain. Mrs. Schaad stated she felt

strange, while watching TV and it felt as if someone was watching them.

Mrs. Schaad stated Mrs. Young had told her that she wanted to get an alarm system for the house. Mrs. Schaad stated Mrs. Young told her that if someone wanted to get inside the home, they were going to no matter what.[i]

 A few weeks earlier, Michelle had called Jason while he was on a business trip in Colorado to tell him she was frightened because she was hearing noises inside the house. Jason told her to call the police. He remembered feeling helpless because he was so far away. Michelle eventually calmed down and shrugged it off. She said the dog wasn't reacting to the sound, so she assumed it was nothing and that was that.
 The house had an alarm system, but the Youngs had not gotten around to activating it. However, after Michelle's scare that night, Jason's step-father gave them a shotgun for protection. They kept it in their bedroom closet. Still, the house was vulnerable. Aside from the non-working alarm system, the garage door opener was broken. Someone could get into the house by manually lifting the garage door, and Michelle never locked the door that led from the garage into the kitchen.
 As planned, Jason stopped for dinner at a Cracker Barrel restaurant in Greensboro, North Carolina. Meredith called him at around nine o'clock while he was enjoying his dinner. She was returning his call from that morning. He wanted to share his side of the story about a recent argument he'd had with Michelle since Meredith was acting as their mediator. They talked for a little over ten minutes and then Jason finished dinner and continued his drive.

Grey's Anatomy was over and Shelly was ready to head home. Michelle had an early doctor appointment the next morning to check on the baby and then planned to head into work. Shelly still felt uneasy so she asked Michelle to walk her to her car. They said good-bye at ten-thirty and Shelly drove off. She did not watch Michelle walk into the house. She had no idea that it would be the last time she would ever see her friend.

Jason decided to stop for the night at a Hampton Inn in Hillsville, Virginia. He arrived at precisely 10:54 p.m. and minutes later checked into room 421. The stop for dinner had made it a four hour trip. He took the elevator to the fourth floor, set down his stuff and called Michelle to let her know he'd arrived safely. Michelle told Jason that Alan would definitely not be coming to visit for the weekend.

Friday, November 3, 2006

Jason woke up early, got showered and dressed, grabbed a quick bite to eat in the lobby, and headed back on Interstate 77. He called his mom at approximately 7:40 a.m. to let her know he would be visiting sometime that afternoon. After hanging up with her, he tried to reach Michelle at home but there was no answer, so he left a message. It was an easy drive along the highway routes—I-77 north to I-81south, but once he got off the highway he became confused with the directions. He had never been to Dickenson Community Hospital and he ended up arriving thirty minutes late. He apologized and they assured him it was okay.

As Jason continued toward his next meeting, he stopped for gas in Duffield, Virginia. He had been having problems with dropped calls, so he made a couple of phone calls after filling up the tank. He spoke to his friend, Bryan Ambrose to firm up their plans for tailgating on Saturday. He had invited Bryan and his family to spend the weekend at their house since they lived pretty far from the stadium. Since Alan Fisher had cancelled his plans to visit that weekend, there was plenty of space for the Ambroses, but Bryan informed Jason that they would spend the night with his in-laws and arrive at the Young's home on Saturday before the game. Since the Ambroses weren't going to spend Friday night with them, that cemented Jason's plan to spend the night at his mom's home in Brevard.

Jason also called Meredith after remembering that he'd accidentally left the print-outs for the Coach purses on the desk. He didn't want Michelle to come home and find them . . . the surprise would be ruined. Meredith didn't answer so he left her a message asking her to go by the house and grab them. He also mentioned that he was going to spend the night in Brevard. He called her shortly after noon as he tried to avoid calling Meredith too early because she usually slept late.

He tried to reach Michelle again both on her cell phone and office phone but was unsuccessful. He knew she was often in meetings, so wasn't too surprised that he was unable to reach her. Jason continued on to Transylvania Community Hospital, and then he would have just a short drive remaining to get to his mom's house.

***

<u>The following is Meredith's account of what happened the afternoon of November 3</u>:

Meredith awoke to the sound of her cell phone ringing at 12:14 p.m. She didn't pick up in time to answer, but immediately retrieved the message from Jason. He'd asked her to pick up the purse print-outs and she planned to eventually get over to the house to do that. First, she wanted to mow the lawn so she put on grubby clothing—a dark sweatshirt and sweatpants and attempted to mow the lawn. She had difficulty operating the mower since mulch had recently been placed in the yard. The lawn mower cut off, so she gave up on the lawn and put the mower back in the garage. She placed a quick (forty-five second) call to her mom at 12:45p.m. Linda returned her call at 1:07 p.m. as Meredith was driving to Michelle's to pick up the print-outs. They talked for just over five minutes. Meredith said that she was pulling into Michelle's driveway just as she was hanging up with Linda. It would have been 1:13 p.m.

Meredith immediately noticed the pillar lights were on. It struck her as odd because Michelle always turned those lights off before going to bed. As she proceeded up the driveway, she noticed that the fence gate was open. When she got out of the car, she approached the gate and noticed there was water running in the backyard spigot. Meredith noted that the opened gate was unusual because it was normally closed to ensure that the dog was secured in the back yard. She didn't turn off the spigot. She attempted to enter the home through the rear garage door entrance, but was unable to open it because large objects were blocking it. She then went to the front door and tried her house key, but it "didn't work." While standing near the front door, she heard the dog "freaking out" inside.

At that point Meredith remembered that the garage door could be manually lifted because the opener was broken, so she walked back over to the garage, raised the door part-way, and proceeded inside. There was never any indication that Meredith considered simply leaving the home, even though things didn't look right and her house key wasn't working. Were the print-outs Jason had asked her to pick up that important? Should she have phoned Michelle and Jason at that point?

Upon raising the garage door, Meredith was surprised to see Michelle's Lexus SUV inside. Michelle was supposed to be at work; Cassidy at daycare. Again, wouldn't it have been a good idea to call someone with yet another unusual circumstance? She continued into the house through the door that led into the kitchen. There she noticed Michelle's purse—a Prada "knock-off" that Meredith had recently given her, tipped over on the floor.

Meredith walked through the foyer and up the stairs to the second floor and called Michelle's name several times, but received no response. Near the top of the stairs she noticed red footprints in Cassidy's bathroom to the right. (She was somehow able to see inside the bathroom, even though the light was off and there was no window in that room.) Her immediate thought was that Cassidy had gotten into Michelle's hair dye. She proceeded up the stairs and turned left into the master bedroom. There she found her sister face-down between the left side of the bed and closet. Her initial thought was that it was a joke, but ruled that out after seeing

Michelle on her stomach. She would not lie that way since she was pregnant.

Cassidy's baby doll and blanket were beside Michelle's body. Blood was spattered on the walls and smeared on the bed. In a panic, she opted to grab a phone before checking on Michelle. She set her sunglasses on the bed and proceeded immediately to the house phone on the night stand at the opposite side of the bed. Just as she got through to the 911 dispatcher, Cassidy popped out from beneath the blankets and latched onto her like a koala bear.

The dispatcher heard the chilling words "I think my sister is dead!" He then instructed Meredith to go to Michelle and turn her over to attempt CPR, but oddly Meredith was more focused on shielding Cassidy from the scene than aiding her sister . . . even though Cassidy would have already seen everything, having been alone in the house for several hours.

The operator told Meredith to secure Cassidy somewhere so she could help Michelle. She told Cassidy to go to her room, at which point the operator told Meredith that she really needed to attempt CPR. She said she was unable to turn Michelle over because she was "twisted in an odd way and was too heavy to move." The operator insisted that she had to try. At that point Meredith stated that Michelle was cold and stiff—it was clear she was gone.

Meredith remained on the line and walked outside with Cassidy and the dog to wait for help. By then the dispatcher had forwarded communications to the Wake County Sheriff's Office. She was told to wait in her car, but she couldn't remember what she'd done with her keys. A fire truck arrived and the call ended. The entire 911 transcript is worth reading to understand Meredith's lack of urgency with regard to trying to save her sister's life. The strangest comments have been underlined by this author.

911 Call Transcript

Operator: 911, location of your emergency?
Meredith: I need an ambulance.
Operator: Okay.
Meredith: It's an emergency.
Operator: What address are you at, Ma'am?
Meredith: Um, Birchleaf. 5108 Birchleaf Road.
Operator: Ma'am, what's your phone number in case I lose you?
Meredith: Oh, my God.
Operator: Okay, what's your phone number?
Meredith: Hang on, let me look at the phone, um, 832-8939.
Operator: Alright, what's the problem? Tell me exactly what happened?
Meredith: I think my sister is dead.
Operator: Okay, tell me what happened, ma'am?
Meredith: I have no idea. Oh, my God.
Operator: Alright. Stay on the phone with me, please. What's your name?
Meredith: Meredith Fisher
Operator: Meredith
Meredith: And this is the Young address. Oh, my God.
Operator: Meredith, listen to me, please.
Meredith: Yeah.
Operator: Are you with the patient now?
Meredith: Yeah, and her daughter, she's —
Operator: Okay, how old is the patient?
Meredith: And there's blood everywhere. She's 28 – 29.
Operator: 28?
Meredith: Should I try to move her?
Operator: Listen to me, ma'am.
Meredith: Yeah. Okay.

Operator: I'm going to tell you what to do.
Meredith: Okay.
Operator: You need to calm down so we can help her. You said there's blood everywhere?
Meredith: Yes.
Operator: Alright. Is she conscious?
Meredith: No, <u>I don't think so</u>. <u>Should I try to help her</u>?
Operator: Listen to me ma'am.
Meredith: I'm listening.
Operator: Is she breathing?
Meredith: <u>I don't think so</u>.
Operator: Have you checked?
Meredith: Michelle? . . . She's cold.
Operator: Okay, listen to me. Did you see what happened?
Meredith: <u>I don't know</u>. Cassidy, come here, sweetie. I'm here with her daughter.
Operator: Okay.
Meredith: There's, there's like blood footprints all over the house from her daughter's little footprints.
Operator: Okay, listen to me. What's your first name?
Meredith: Meredith
Operator: Alright, Meredith.
Meredith: Yes, sir.
Operator: Did you see what happened?
Meredith: I, I, I just came here on a <u>fluke</u>. I usually, you know, don't come here during the day.
Operator: Okay.
Meredith: She shouldn't be home. She should be at work like —
Operator: Okay, listen to me.
Meredith: Yes, sir.
Cassidy: Emmie, Emmie.

Meredith: I'm on the phone right now.

Operator: Did you say — can you tell me why it looks like she's dead?

Meredith: <u>I don't know. I have no idea.</u> There's blood all over the place.

Operator: Did you say she's cold?

Meredith: Yeah.

Operator: Okay.

Meredith: Yes.

Operator: Alright. Stay on the phone.

Meredith: Okay.

Cassidy: Emmie, Emmie there's blood. Did you see my . . . can you get a washcloth from . . . ?

Meredith: Yeah, sweetie. (Inaudible) <u>Do you know what happened to Mommy? Did she fall</u>?

Cassidy: Um she got a boo — she got boo boos everywhere and and she got —

Operator: Alright. Do you think she's beyond any help?

Meredith: <u>I don't know honestly</u>.

Operator: You don't know, alright.

Meredith: I'm normally very good under pressure. I'm just like (inaudible)

Operator: We're going to tell you what to do, okay?

Meredith: Yes, sir.

Operator: Are you right by her now?

Meredith: <u>I'm keeping her daughter out of there</u>.

Operator: Okay, so you're not with her?

Meredith: <u>I'm, I'm right outside the bedroom</u>.

Operator: Alright. Can you get her daughter secured so — can you carry the phone in to where she's at?

Meredith: Yes.

Operator: Alright. Can you secure her daughter?
Meredith: Cassidy, sweetie, can you stay in your room for two seconds, okay?
Operator: Meredith.
Meredith: Okay. Yes, sir.
Operator: Okay, have you got a cordless phone?
Meredith: Yes.
Operator: Alright.
Meredith: Stay there sweetie, okay?
Operator: Alright. Is she on — is she laying on her back?
Meredith: No, she's laying on her stomach.
Operator: She's on her stomach. She's face down?
Meredith: Yes.
Operator: Alright. Can you get her on her back?
Meredith: Okay. Oh my God. Michelle? <u>I don't think so</u>, she's so heavy.
Operator: Let's see if you can get her on her back.
Meredith: I really think she's dead.
Operator: Pardon?
Meredith: I really think she's dead.
Operator: Okay, are you certain?
Meredith: <u>Hang on. Cassidy, sweetie, please go in your room. Kay, honey</u>? Um, I'm pretty sure.
Operator: You are?
Meredith: <u>No, I don't know</u>. I'm, I'm —
Operator: Okay. We need to make sure.
Meredith: Okay.
Operator: Can you get her on her back for me?
Meredith: She's kind of twisted in a, in a way that I can't do that.
Operator: You can't roll her over?
Meredith: <u>No, not easily</u>.

19

Operator: You're going to have to try.

Meredith: Hang on. Let me — I'm trying to see if I can get her pulse.

Operator: We've got to try to do CPR if we can get her on her back, Meredith.

Meredith: No, she's ice cold.

Operator: She's cold?

Meredith: Yes.

Operator: Okay. Alright.

Meredith: Her body is stiff.

Operator: Okay. Then don't try. If she's cold then let's —

Meredith: Oh, my God, I don't know what happened to her. <u>Should I not touch anything</u>?

Operator: There's probably nothing else that you can do.

Operator: Alright. Try not to touch anything more than you did. Was anything out of place or unusual when you came in?

Meredith: <u>This place does not look like what it normally looks like</u>.

Operator: Okay, What —

Meredith: There is blood in the bed.

Operator: Okay. Alright. Try not to touch anything else, okay?

Meredith: <u>Okay, I just moved a pillow</u>.

Operator: Just leave everything exactly where it is then.

Meredith: Okay. Okay.

Operator: Do you see anything else?

Meredith: Um

Operator: Do you see anything else that looks unusual?

Meredith: No. Cassidy, was anybody here? The dog was freaking out when I got here. Was anybody here, sweetie?

Cassidy: (inaudible)

Operator: Alright. I'm going to get the Sheriff's Department to pick up on the line with us.

Meredith: Okay.

Operator: They're going to need to talk to you about what you're seeing, okay?

Meredith: Okay.

Operator: I'm going to brief them on what's happened and you just stay on the line. What's your last name, Meredith?

Meredith: Fisher. Her last name is Young.

Operator: Are you her relative?

Meredith: I'm her only sister.

Operator: Okay. Alright, Meredith. Stay with me just a minute, okay?

Meredith: Okay.

WCSO Operator: Sheriff's Office. What is your emergency?

Operator: Hey, this is Brent.

WCSO: Uh-huh.

Operator: Look, I've got a lady named Meredith Fisher on the line from this address.

WCSO: Okay.

Operator: And she's in there with her sister. Um, she's going to tell you about what she's seen and it's apparent it might be a code seven and there may be — there is evidence of trauma.

WCSO: We've got deputies already en route.

Operator: Okay. Do you want to talk to her? I'm going to let her talk to you.

WCSO: I will. Thanks.

Operator: She's on line with you.

WCSO: Okay.

Operator: Meredith, go ahead.

WCSO: Meredith.

Meredith: I'm also here with — her two-and-a-half year old, so it's kind of difficult for me to pay attention.

WCSO: Okay.

Meredith: Okay.

WCSO: Where are you at now, though, Meredith? You're on Birchleaf?

Meredith: Downstairs on — at 5108 Birchleaf.

WCSO: Okay.

Meredith: Um I typically handle myself very well under pressure, but I don't know what to do.

WCSO: Okay. Now, is rescue there yet?

Meredith: No.

WCSO: Okay.

Meredith: Should I go outside and wait for them so they —

WCSO: Now what have you found when you walked into the house?

Meredith: I don't know. <u>I almost thought it was a practical joke</u>. There's just blood everywhere.

WCSO: Okay, who lives there and are they there?

Meredith: Okay, it's my sister's house.

WCSO: Uh-huh.

Meredith: And she has a husband that travels quite a bit.

WCSO: Uh-huh.

Meredith: Um, I spoke with him last night. He's out of town. He's on his way to his parent's house. And her daughter that's still in pajamas —

WCSO: Okay

Meredith: Normally my sister goes to work early and takes her to daycare, you know like . . . something's not right. <u>And when I first came to the house</u> —

WCSO: Could you hold on one second for me?

Meredith: Yes, sir.

WCSO: Ma'am?

Meredith: Yes, sir.

WCSO: Okay. Are you — are you out at the deceased person at Birch Leaf?

Meredith: I'm sorry?

WCSO: Are you out on Birch Leaf?

Meredith: Birch Leaf; yes, sir.

WCSO: Okay. What I need you to do if possible — who all is there with you? I can hear a child.

Meredith: Yeah.

WCSO: Okay. EMS and I got some deputies en route, but what I need you to go ahead and do is just walk outside.

Meredith: Okay.

WCSO: Because we don't know what is going on yet. Just have everybody walk outside, stand — (inaudible)

Meredith: Let's take a ride, okay? Come on, Garrison (Youngs' dog). Let's go, Buddy.

Cassidy: Where are we going?

Meredith: We're going to go outside and wait for nice people to visit.

WCSO: If you want to go ahead out — go out to your car and sit in your car. That way — until we figure out what's going on, okay?

Meredith: Okay. I don't know what I did with my keys. I can't even think.

Cassidy: Where are we going?

Meredith: We're going outside to wait for a nice police officer to come talk to us, okay, sweetie?

WCSO: Who is this person to you?

Meredith: This is my niece that I'm holding right now.

WCSO: No, I mean the person in the house.

Meredith: My sister.

Cassidy: Is that your car?

WCSO: Your sister?
Meredith: Oh, my God.
Cassidy: Is that your car?
Meredith: Yes, sweetie, that's my car.
WCSO: Yeah, just, just do the best you can.
Meredith: I'm trying.
WCSO: I know. I know it's difficult. I really do.
Meredith: My niece is very smart for her age. She's two-and-a-half, but I think that she's saying that there was somebody in the house. I don't really understand because I don't . . . I know she doesn't understand.
WCSO: How old is your sister?
Meredith: My sister is 29.
WCSO: 29. Does she have any problems?
Meredith: What?
WCSO: Does she have any personal problems that you know of?
Meredith: Um not really. You know like her and her husband fight a little bit, but nothing too ridiculous. She's pregnant, I know that. She's about four-and-a-half months pregnant.
WCSO: Try, try to keep calm with me, okay?
Meredith: I'm trying.
WCSO: Go ahead and give me a channel.
Meredith: There's a fire department truck here.
WCSO: Okay.
Meredith: I don't know why, but —
WCSO: They respond as well because of the nature of the call.
Meredith: I'm trying. Oh, my God. Oh, my God. I can't believe that this is real. Like the two of them play jokes on each other, like my sister and her husband, like <u>I almost thought it was a joke, that's how over the top it just seems in there that something is not right</u>.

WCSO: Okay. But the fire department is going to talk to you now. They'll probably go in the house to check on her, okay?
Meredith: Okay, thank you.
WCSO: And if — they'll let me know if there's any problems, okay? Just stay out of the house as best as you can okay?
Meredith: Thank you. Yes, thank you.
WCSO: Okay.
Call ended

While it's understandable that Meredith may have been in shock, she didn't even check on Michelle before placing the call. She didn't demand immediate assistance for her sister. She was preoccupied with Cassidy at a time when seconds could have counted. She didn't respond to direct questions. She refused to turn the body over to attempt CPR. Her responses seemed to indicate that she already knew Michelle was dead when she placed the call.

It was also odd that she used the word "fluke" when describing how she'd happened to be there that day. (Fluke: unlikely chance occurrence, especially a surprising piece of luck).

Meredith claimed she called 911 from the house phone on the bedside table. This author recently discovered that the call did not in fact originate from that phone. It is not listed on the phone records, nor is it listed on her cell phone records. What phone was used to place the call? Is it possible the call was placed with a disposable cell phone? Though it is a public record, this author has been unsuccessful at obtaining the 911 call CAD report, which would show the originating number.

Meredith couldn't remember where she'd placed her car keys. Police found them later that day on the hood of Michelle's Lexus. She had no explanation for how they had gotten there. It is difficult to picture a scenario that would account for Meredith placing her keys on the hood of the Lexus.

CHAPTER 2

Jason and Michelle

Jason grew up in Brevard, North Carolina with his mother, Pat and his two sisters Heather and Kimberly. Their father died unexpectedly when Jason was just five years old. His mother began dating Gerald McIntyre when Jason was around seven years old and he shared in the upbringing of the Young children and eventually married Pat.

Friends and family describe Jason as outgoing and fun. Everyone wanted to be around him. He had lots of friends. He always enjoyed sports, camping, boating and hiking and even hiked the Appalachian Trail. He loved to tease people, all in good fun. He also had a sensitive side. His sister Heather recalled how Jason described the birth of Cassidy and how he felt the first time he held her and the two of them began bonding.

Jason and Michelle met at a bar in Raleigh called The Pour House. Michelle was celebrating her birthday and enjoying a glass of wine with friends. Jason was goofing around and spilled Michelle's glass of wine. He apologized and bought her a fresh drink. They began talking and seemed to hit it off from the start. He felt somewhat intimidated when he first met Michelle because he thought she was so pretty and very sweet. He felt like she was a bit out of his league, but they began dating and their relationship soon became serious.

Michelle graduated with an accounting degree and went on to earn her masters. She was a go-getter and completed her master's program in one year. She and Jason decided to move into a townhouse Jason had purchased with his friend, Ryan Schaad. The three of them lived together until Michelle unexpectedly became pregnant. At that point Jason and Michelle decided to get married so Ryan moved out. They were married at the court house on August 12, 2003 but had a traditional wedding ceremony on October 10, 2003.

Michelle with Linda and Meredith

Cassidy was born five months later on March 29, 2004. Jason and Michelle were doing well. Michelle was already working at Progress Energy by then and Jason held a sales position with Pan America Lab. They adored Cassidy and wanted to ensure that she would always be cared for. They discussed who would be the most suitable guardian for her if anything were to happen to them and they decided upon Jason's sister, Heather and her husband,

Joe. They were married and planned on having children of their own some day. Cassidy would have stability with them. Meredith wasn't a good candidate at that time as she was currently single and just getting on her feet. After seeking Heather's and Joe's approval of the guardianship, they drew up a will.

***

Michelle had a difficult childhood growing up in Sayville, New York. Her parents were always fighting and there was a lot of tension in the house. Alan owned a car dealership. Linda was a school teacher and cheerleading coach at Sayville High School. Both of the Fisher girls were cheerleaders, but were a few grades apart in school.

Alan and Linda divorced in 1996 while Michelle was attending NC State. Michelle had never been very close to her father, but their relationship became even more strained when he remarried. Michelle despised his new wife, June and refused to visit their home, but she reconnected with Alan after Cassidy was born. She wanted her daughter to have a close relationship with her grandfather, but she still refused to speak to June. Jason got along well with both Alan and June and often encouraged Michelle to resolve her issues with June, but it never happened.

Michelle didn't get along with her sister growing up. They would often fight and it even got physical at times—they would bite and scratch each other. They were very different people. Michelle was thin, pretty and popular. She had lots of friends and created a successful life for herself. Meredith seemed to struggle. She struggled with her weight and according to police interviews, there were rumors she was involved in drugs off and on. Some of Michelle's friends believed she was jealous of her older sister.

Even into adulthood, there were conflicts in their relationship. An undated note from Linda was found in the house after Michelle's death. It described how Meredith had ruined Thanksgiving and that Michelle needed to learn how to talk to her sister.

> Dear Michelle,
> I have a couple of minutes and I wanted to tell you how much I enjoyed talking to you about Meredith. I just want to remind you that no one likes to be told <u>what</u> to do, so the <u>way</u> you say things will definitely make a difference. I hope by the time Christmas vacation rolls around <u>hopefully</u> things will be a lot better than Thanksgiving. I wish she would on her own, not with your help admit to the *disaster* of Thanksgiving and hopefully we could have a family Christmas!
>
> Mom

The letter illustrates the tension between the sisters. Perhaps there was much more to the relationship than is known. Whatever the case, it's clear they didn't always get along.

***

There was a bizarre murder case that occurred in Sayville while Meredith was a senior in high school. Seventeen year old Charity Miranda was <u>murdered</u> by her mother and sister in a ritualistic ceremony. Meredith, a classmate and member of the same cheerleading squad as the victim, is pictured to the left of Charity in this photo.

Katie Schaum, Keri Mckenna, Melissa Eccles, Jessica Duggan, Meredith Fisher, Charity Miranda, Jaimie Wallace, Lori Reiser, Tara Slochower, Jodi Baker, Marissa Bracco, Joyce Haggerty, Michelle Penyy.

After Charity was killed, her mother and sister moved the body to the stairwell to make it look like an accidental death. It was believed to be a Santeria sacrifice. There are several instances of Santeria animal sacrifices in the United States—animal heads will be found, sometimes with food or notes or money, but human sacrifice such as Charity's tragic slaying is rare. It is quite a coincidence that Meredith's life was touched twice by murder.

Another equally bizarre connection is the television program, Sabrina the Teenage Witch. Actress Melissa Joan Hart attended Sayville High School with Michelle Fisher before becoming famous for her lead role in the program. The premise of the show was that Sabrina cast spells on her arch enemy—a popular cheerleader. Michelle was a cheerleader in the same graduating class as Melissa Joan Hart.

CHAPTER 3

Coping with the news

Meredith hung up with the 911operator just after exiting the house on that horrible day. By then a fire truck had arrived so she took Cassidy to sit inside the truck to keep warm while waiting for help to arrive. They were unable to sit in Meredith's car because she couldn't remember where she'd placed her car keys. Upon the discovery that Cassidy had been alone for several hours, paramedic Scott Hughes stopped by to check her vital signs. Everything was fine. She was surprisingly calm and had no visible blood on her, despite evidence that she'd smeared blood on the walls and left tiny bloody footprints in the hall bathroom. It seemed obvious that someone had cleaned her up. Years later Hughes would tell ADA Becky Holt that he believed Meredith said she'd cleaned Cassidy up, but he couldn't be certain. He did not grasp the significance of the accuracy of that recollection.

While holding Cassidy on her hip, Meredith stepped out of the fire truck and made some phone calls. She called her roommate, Colleen. She also called her mom, but didn't have a chance to tell her about Michelle. Linda told her she would have to call her back because she was getting her hair done, which was very odd. Why didn't Meredith say "It's an emergency, mom!"?

Deputy Earp of the Wake County Sheriff's Office was one of the first police officers to arrive at the scene. While securing the inside of the house, he noticed a huge amount of blood near the body and small bloody footprints on the bathroom floor. After exiting the house, he observed Meredith and Cassidy stepping out of the fire truck. He noted that Meredith did not appear to be upset, but as soon as the detective arrived to speak to her, she became upset and appeared to be crying. Like Hughes, he too was surprised that he didn't see any blood on Cassidy.

> "I observed an adult white female exit a fire truck carrying a white female child. One of the firemen advised me this was the sister-in-law and the victim's child. They approached me and I asked the adult female if the child had been cleaned and she replied 'no.' I was expecting her to reply yes, because while in the house I noticed child footprints in blood on the second floor hallway bathroom, and at this time the child did not appear to have any blood on her. I noticed the child *wearing socks* and the footprints I saw were bare feet. I also observed blood smear marks on the same bathroom wall about hand level to this child. I did not see any blood on the child's hands during our encounter.[ii]

Meredith told police that Cassidy was found in bare feet, which was inconsistent with Deputy Earp's observation. The deputy typed up his summary that same day, so his account was certainly reliable. By Meredith's account, she wouldn't have had time to clean Cassidy's hands and feet or change her clothing. She claimed that she placed the 911 call as soon as she arrived at the house, and found Cassidy "shockingly clean." That can only mean that the killer(s) or those who had knowledge of the crime cleaned her up. Would detectives understand the significance of Cassidy's condition?

After speaking to Deputy Earp, Meredith took Cassidy to the Gilgens' house to use the bathroom. Laura and David Gilgen lived next door to the Youngs with their thirteen year old daughter and fifteen year old son. David met them at the driveway and carried Cassidy to the first floor bathroom, at which point he noticed she was *not* wearing socks, which was odd because the deputy had just seen her in socks. David ran upstairs to grab a pair of his daughter's socks for the child, even though the adult-sized socks were much too large for her. It was a chilly afternoon and she needed something on her feet.

While Cassidy was in the bathroom, Laura asked Meredith if she was okay, and she shook her head and said "no" and began crying when Laura hugged her. As soon as David returned with Cassidy, she immediately stopped crying. She seemed to turn her tears off and on at will. Meredith did not ask the Gilgens for food or water for Cassidy, even though she would have been alone in the house for several hours, having last eaten the night before.

While all of this was happening, Jason was en route to Transylvania Community Hospital to visit his final customer of the day. His cell phone reception was so poor that he didn't know if Meredith had even received his message about picking up the Coach print-outs, so he phoned his mom and asked her to leave a message for Meredith. Pat did call and leave a message. Little did she know that at that very moment Meredith was standing in the front lawn of the Birchleaf home with police, paramedics, and firemen swarming all over the property.

Meredith would later state that she didn't have her cell phone that afternoon because she had left it in the car, which was now part of the crime scene. For the time being, she was using the hand set phone from the house. Interestingly, cell phone usage was documented on her records long before the car was released by police, and even the very afternoon that Michelle was found. Investigators never seemed to note that inconsistency. She was either lying, or she somehow retrieved the phone from her car that day. It's also possible she had the cell phone in her possession the entire time, but why would she lie about something like that?

Meredith attempted to reach her mother a second time. This time she supposedly told her "Michele is d-e-a-d" as Linda was driving home from her hair appointment. Oddly, the call lasted only two and a half minutes. One would expect a lengthier call given the shocking news she would have just received, but Linda didn't waste any time. Just six minutes later, she called Jason from her home phone and left a message for him to call her back immediately. Next, she called Pat Young and told her "My Michelle is dead."

The news was so shocking that Pat called Meredith to find out if it was true. Meredith sounded so calm that she assumed it must have been a mistake, but Meredith did confirm that Michelle was indeed dead. Meredith told Pat that she couldn't talk long because detectives wanted to speak with her. Since Meredith provided so few details, Pat was left wondering if Michelle's death was related to some type of problem with the pregnancy. Meredith did not tell her that Michelle may have been murdered, even though it should have been quite obvious based on the bloody scene.

At some point, Colleen arrived at the Birchleaf home. Meredith instantly placed Cassidy in her car and told her "Michelle is d-e-a-d." She didn't give Colleen a chance to ask any questions. She just told her to take care of Cassidy while she talked to the police. Meredith would later describe that she was spelling out the word dead because Cassidy was with her.

At approximately 3:45 p.m., Deputy Donna Tanner took Meredith and Cassidy to Target because Cassidy needed a change of clothing and something to eat. Tanner asked Cassidy some questions during the drive —

> On 11-3-06 at approximately 3:44 p.m., myself, Meredith Fisher and 2 ½ year old Cassidy Young left 5108 Birchleaf Drive and went to Target on Walnut Street in Cary, NC. Cassidy needed some food and some clean clothes because the crime scene was secure.
>
> Cassidy said her Daddy took her to school yesterday (11-2-06) morning and her mom picked her up from school yesterday afternoon. Cassidy said her "Aunt Shelly" came by her house yesterday. Cassidy told me she did not walk the dog (Mr. G.) today.
>
> Meredith advised "Aunt Shelly" was a friend of her late sister. Meredith said Cassidy was saying "Go away, go away" on this date when she arrived at her sister's house. Meredith advised she does not know who Cassidy was talking about.
>
> When I asked "Cassie" what happened to her mom she did not answer. I asked her who hurt her mom. She did not answer. All she would say was her mom was dead. She looked at me but did not answer. She never mentioned her dad after she told me he took her to school on Thursday.

I did not observe any blood or any type of stains on Cassie's clothing she was wearing. She had on a matching fleece outfit. *She was wearing socks* but no shoes.[iii]

It's interesting that Meredith told the deputy that Cassidy said, "Go away" when she'd arrived at the house. That is inconsistent with Cassidy popping up from under the blanket as Meredith was placing the call to 911. Cassidy wasn't heard at all at that point.

It's worth noting that Deputy Tanner also observed Cassidy wearing socks, yet made no mention that the socks were way too large for her. Both Tanner and Earp observed her wearing socks, yet Meredith claimed that she was found in bare feet. This is very significant because Cassidy was unable to put socks on by herself, so if she was found in clean socks, it indicates that someone put them on her after cleaning the blood off her feet.

Two of Cassidy's bloody socks were found on the bath mat in the hall bathroom; one of Cassidy's clean white socks was found in the upstairs hallway. It is unfortunate that investigators didn't spend more time looking into whether or not Cassidy was wearing socks when she was found. They simply accepted Meredith's statement that she was found in bare feet; despite two officers who'd observed her wearing socks.

When they arrived at Target, Meredith took Cassidy into the store while Tanner waited in her patrol car. Colleen had followed in her car to help. Meredith bought diapers and fresh clothes for Cassidy, changed her in the restroom and later gave police the clothing Cassidy had been wearing when she was found—except that she didn't turn over the pink t-shirt or the socks from the

Gilgens. It is unclear why she didn't give them all of the clothing at that time.

Police wouldn't learn of the missing t-shirt and socks until a later interview with Shelly Schaad. Shelly was asked to describe what Cassidy was wearing that night. Following that interview, police asked Meredith about the missing pink t-shirt and she informed them that she had it at her home and had washed it. She explained that she left it on Cassidy when she changed her at Target.

It's unfortunate that Deputy Tanner didn't go into the store with them to ensure that all of the clothing items were collected, but at that time police had no idea how significant these details would be. As it stands, there is no way to know if Cassidy was wearing the t-shirt when her clothing was changed at Target. If she wasn't, it would prove Meredith's involvement in the crime or at least in the caring and clean-up of Cassidy during the several hours when she was presumed to be alone in the house. It's known that Cassidy was wearing the same pajama top that Michelle dressed her in the night before and she wasn't capable of removing her t-shirt and then putting her shirt back on herself.

Police added the pink t-shirt to the evidence logs in sequence with the other clothing items, never noting that the t-shirt had been separated from Cassidy's other clothing items and that it hadn't been collected until weeks later.

***

Meanwhile, Linda left Jason a second message to inform him that she had booked a 5:30 p.m. flight to Raleigh. She then called Cassidy's pediatrician to inform him about Michelle's death and request advice about how to handle Cassidy. The call lasted thirteen minutes. She would later tell Jason and his family that the doctor said that Cassidy would be fine as long as nobody asked her any questions about what had happened. This would prove to be a mistake, as the child was quite verbal. Experts should have interviewed her that very day to find out what she may have seen or heard.

Pat Young and her husband Gerald were waiting for Jason to arrive at their home. They were naturally very upset and tense about having to share the devastating news with Jason. They agreed that he needed to hear about Michelle in person, as it would be unsafe for him to drive after receiving such shocking news. So they waited.

Jason was heading home after his final meeting for the day. He was probably thinking about the weekend ahead and looking forward to getting together with friends for the NC State game. He could have never anticipated that his life was about to be permanently shattered. He pulled into the driveway of his mother's home at around three o'clock, got out of the car and greeted the dog. At that time, Pat and Gerald came outside and Jason could tell something was wrong. He instantly thought it was his elderly grandmother, but no. There was no easy way to tell him, so Gerald came straight out and said "Michelle is dead." Jason dropped to his knees in shock and disbelief. He was helped inside and comforted as best as possible.

Pat knew they had to get to Raleigh as soon as possible so she called Jason's sister, Heather and his brother-in-law, Joe to inform them about Michelle and to ask if they could travel to Raleigh with her and Jason. She knew Jason was in no condition to drive. Heather and Joe, shocked at the news, agreed to make the trip to Raleigh with them. They hurriedly packed their bags and got to the house as soon as possible. They decided to drive together in Jason's Explorer, so the four of them—Jason, Pat, Heather and Joe packed up the vehicle and headed to Raleigh. Joe drove, Heather sat up front with him, and Jason sat in the back with his mom.

Jason called Colleen's cell phone during the drive, hoping to speak to Meredith. Jason spoke to Meredith very briefly and did not ask a lot of questions. He mainly wanted to know what Cassidy needed, and then he handed the phone to Pat. Meredith could hear Jason crying while speaking with Pat.

Meredith shared more details with Pat at that time. She mentioned that there was blood everywhere and that Cassidy had placed her baby doll face down next to Michelle and placed band-aids all over Michelle's body. She also said that Michelle's purse had been turned over with all the contents spilled out on the counter-top. What could have possibly happened to Michelle? Pat didn't know what to make of the information Meredith had just shared and it was all very upsetting.

Later, a police officer from the Wake County Sheriff's Office called Pat and asked "Where are you?" and then, "Is Jason with you? He better be!" Police had already visited some of Jason's and Michelle's friends by then, prompted by Meredith's statement to Deputy Tanner. She told her that Shelly Schaad had been visiting with Michelle the prior evening. Police went to Shelly's home that afternoon to ask her questions since she may have been one of the last people to see Michelle alive. Shelly was married to Ryan Schaad—Jason's close friend and former roommate from college days. Ryan was present during Shelly's interview and was concerned with the line of questioning. Police were already suspicious of Jason. Ryan had to call Jason to let him know.

Jason received Ryan's call when they were just a short distance from Meredith's home. Ryan told him that he needed to hire an attorney before speaking to police because he was clearly under suspicion. They pulled into an Applebee's restaurant near Meredith's home so they could figure out what to do. Jason did not know any attorneys, so Heather began making some calls to see if she could help him find an attorney. Jason made the decision that he would not speak to the police until he'd had a chance to consult with an attorney.

It was very late when they finally arrived at Meredith's. Colleen had picked Linda up from the airport that evening, so she was already there. Meredith's boyfriend, "Shai" was there also. Everyone called him Shai, but his real name was Olusegun Olusesi. He was a medical student at the University of North Carolina. They had met through a Craigslist ad placed by Meredith.

Jason got out of the car, hugged Meredith, and then went straight to Cassidy. He sought comfort from Cassidy and he knew she needed comfort too. She would be missing her mother.

While Jason was in the bedroom with Cassidy, police called to speak with him, but he refused. On a side note, this is a touchy situation because most attorneys advise clients to avoid speaking to police if they are suspected of a crime. It is easy for statements to be twisted or even fabricated if the interview isn't recorded. It is a smart move to hire an attorney before speaking to police, but unfortunately police sometimes view silence as guilt and assume the person must be hiding something. In turn, that sometimes motivates police to focus solely on that person when they could be missing important clues that point elsewhere. There really is no perfect way to handle a situation such as this. It's probably safest to hire a lawyer but agree to at least answer written questions from police, or better yet agree to an interview with police but only with an attorney present. This will ensure that one has provided all the information necessary to rule one out as a suspect and share details that may be helpful to the investigation. For example, Jason could have told police that he and Michelle had recently been hearing noises at night.

***

The mood in the house was somber. How does one cope with something like this? While Jason was with Cassidy, everyone else sat and talked in the living room as they tried to piece together what had happened. Heather and Pat recalled feeling uncomfortable as Meredith and Shai had a matter-of-fact conversation about the height of the blood spatter while speculating about whether Michelle may have fallen. How could Meredith have even considered that Michelle had fallen after seeing that scene?

Colleen told Heather that when Meredith called and asked her to come to the Birchleaf house she didn't want to go, but Meredith *made her* go. Why would she not want to go and help her friend? It was very odd . . . as well as suspicious. Did Colleen know something?

Ryan and Shelly Schaad stopped by Meredith's home late that evening to check on Jason. Meredith began asking Shelly questions in an accusatory tone. Meredith said she didn't know Shelly was going to be at the house that evening. She also asked Shelly if Michelle had taken a shower, because she thought Michelle's hair looked wet. This was a very odd question . . . her hair was wet due to the blood, and even if Michelle did have wet hair that night, surely it would have been dry by the time Meredith found her the next afternoon!

Meredith gave police inconsistent statements about her knowledge of Shelly's presence at the Birchleaf home that evening. She initially told Deputy Tanner that Shelly had been there, which prompted the police visit; however, two days later she would tell lead detective Brent David that she was *unaware* that Shelly had been there, as Michelle hadn't mentioned it when they'd spoken on the phone that evening. Why the inconsistency? Why was Meredith attempting to conceal her knowledge that Shelly was there that night? Police didn't seem to care or notice.

***

It was after midnight on a very stressful and emotional day that would never be forgotten. Joe and Heather were exhausted and decided to grab their suitcases from the Explorer and somehow get to a hotel for some rest. Suddenly police pulled up and told them to put the suitcases back in the vehicle. They asked Heather where Jason was and she told them he was inside the house with his daughter. They asked her "Is there any way he can escape out the back?" She couldn't believe the question. At that point they seized the vehicle and everything in it, including all the luggage, purses, cell phones and even medications. Heather, Joe and Pat were taken to the police station for questioning, which lasted into the early morning hours. Pat was the only one of the three questioned at that time.

Meredith was also escorted separately to the police station for questioning. Detective David interviewed her at that time. He asked Meredith why she went to the house. She explained that she'd received a call from Jason with a request to pick up some print-outs. In describing the experience of finding her sister dead, she mentioned that Michelle's eyesight was very poor and that she would have needed her glasses to see if she'd removed her contacts before bed. She also pointed out that Michelle was not dressed for bed—she was wearing a hooded sweatshirt. This information seemed to point toward the murder having occurred before Michelle went to bed, so likely before midnight.

Meredith also informed the detective that the heat was not working on the second floor of the Birchleaf home. She told him that Michelle had a history of depression and some marital problems. When asked about Jason's reluctance to talk to them, she told him that Jason said he would talk to police, but only with an attorney present. She said she did not observe any injuries on him. She told the detective that she spoke to Jason approximately one hour after finding Michelle dead, but that wasn't true based on the phone records. She hadn't called Jason at all that afternoon. Police did not ask Meredith any questions about her whereabouts the night of the murder. Colleen picked her up shortly after four a.m. and drove her home.

At approximately the same time, Ryan Schaad picked up Pat, Heather and Joe from the police station, since they were now without a vehicle. They were taken to get something to eat and then to a hotel. Since everything from the Explorer had been seized, they didn't even have a credit card to pay for the hotel room. Was it really necessary? Couldn't police have allowed the women to have their purses? Ryan had to take care of the expenses for them at that time. He also let them borrow one of his cars. They were grateful for his support at that difficult time. Jason and Cassidy spent the night at Meredith's as it was quiet with everyone but Linda at the police station.

The next morning Jason said he was planning to ask his friends to try to get some of his clothing from the house, since he had nothing but the clothes on his back. Meredith said that he wouldn't want to do that because "the closet was a mess and most of the murder had taken place there." This was yet another very odd statement. She shouldn't have had time to look in the closet if she'd called 911 as soon as she found Michelle. As well, she seemed to have become convinced all of a sudden that Michelle had been murdered, after speculating the night before that Michelle may have fallen and hit her head. So many of her statements were odd and should have been red flags, but police felt so certain that Jason was their suspect, that Meredith's inconsistencies didn't raise red flags . . . at least not initially. The failure to consider Meredith a suspect caused police to overlook many things along the way.

By Sunday, more relatives of the Fisher's had arrived at Meredith's house, so Jason, Cassidy, Joe, Heather and Pat went to stay with Jason's other sister, Kim and her husband, Stephen at their farm house in Aberdeen. At some point that day police delivered word to the families that Michelle had been murdered, though no specific details were given. Of course, everyone had pretty much figured that out by then, based on the types of questions police had asked during the interviews. Still, it was shocking and devastating to hear it.

Though it hadn't been released to the public, Dr. Thomas Clark performed an autopsy the day after Michelle was found. He determined that Michelle had died as a result of blunt force trauma to the head. She sustained multiple lacerations to the head, a broken jaw, and a skull fracture. The impact was strong enough to knock out some of her teeth. There were defensive wounds on her hands. Fingernail marks on the side of her neck were an indication that someone had also tried to strangle her.

Michelle was dressed in a white t-shirt, black pants and a zipped-up hooded sweatshirt—not clothing she would typically wear to bed, though it appeared the attack may have started in the bed based on the presence of blood. Her contacts had been removed. The time of death was estimated to be between midnight and six a.m.

***

Meredith went to the sheriff's office on Sunday afternoon for a more thorough interview. At that time, she began feeding police information that seemed to cast suspicion on Jason. She talked about the value of the couple's life insurance policies. She suggested that Jason had an online gambling problem. She described a car accident that had occurred the previous summer and suggested that Jason may have intentionally wrecked the car. She stated that the arguments between the two had become more frequent.

Meredith was finally asked about her whereabouts the night of the murder.

<u>The following is Meredith's account from the night of November 2 — morning of November 3</u> (source: police reports)

(9:00 p.m. – 2:00 a.m.)
Upon completing her shift at Lucky 32, Meredith called Jason at approximately nine o'clock while en route to the Carolina Ale House to meet her friend, Betsy for drinks. She was returning his call from that morning. Jason had called Meredith to discuss his side of a recent argument he'd had with Michelle. Specifically, he had overheard Michelle talking on the phone to Linda, claiming he had thrown a remote at her. Jason insisted that it wasn't true, that he did not throw the remote and he wanted Meredith to know that since she was the acting mediator of their conflicts. They talked for about ten minutes.

After ending the call with Jason, Meredith met Betsy at the Carolina Ale House and remained there until last call at two a.m. She then sat in Betsy's car for a few minutes and talked, wanting to allow for some time to sober up since she had consumed approximately five drinks. She told Betsy she was considering going to Michelle's house to spend the night since her home was just a short drive from the Ale House, but she told police she did not end up going to Michelle's—that she felt sober enough to drive the whole way home.

(2:15-3 a.m.)
Meredith called her roommate, Colleen on her way home to see if she was awake. She decided to stop at a Sheetz store to buy a pretzel and pack of cigarettes, then arrived home at around three a.m. and went to sleep. So it was now clear that Meredith was out very late. Would police do everything possible to verify her whereabouts?

***

Everyone was doing their best to ensure that Cassidy had all the support she needed during this difficult time. Despite the trauma she would have endured from finding her mother dead, she was doing very well. There were no signs of distress and it seemed unlikely she'd witnessed the murder. She told her Aunt Kim, "Mommy was Sleeping Beauty." She also said she was eating jelly beans and watching the Lion King in the Barbie room with Emmy. Cassidy called Meredith "Emmy." Cassidy also said something about a "Fancy" and a Mulan in her bedroom—possibly a reference from the Disney Mulan movie? Fancy may have been Cassidy's word for "fantasy," but it was difficult to know. It would have been helpful for police to bring in a child psychologist to question Cassidy about what she saw, but it never happened.

Jason complied with a request from police to submit to a non-testimonial order to be examined and provide fingerprints and a DNA sample on November 8—five days after Michelle was found dead. An examination of his body revealed no scratches or marks.

Funeral arrangements were made over the next couple of days, amid obvious tension between Jason and Linda. Linda insisted on an open casket despite the visible damage to Michelle's face. She wanted her daughter to look beautiful. Jason preferred to leave that decision up to the funeral director. They knew their limitations. Ultimately he decided it was best to allow Linda to handle the arrangements, but offered to pay for everything and gave Linda his credit card number.

Michelle's father, Alan Fisher was planning to bring June to the funeral. Linda and Meredith were adamantly opposed to it. Michelle hated June, so the Fisher women did not want her there and they were unwilling to budge. Jason stood up for June and felt it was inappropriate to create drama over this. Alan was grieving the loss of his daughter and had a right to have his wife at his side for comfort. Linda and Meredith were angry with Jason for not siding with them on this. A clear line was drawn.

The funeral took place on Wednesday November 9. Jason was holding it together the best that he could. His family was by his side. He couldn't even go to the casket alone. They all decided to go together. Jason lightly patted Michelle's tummy, thinking about the son he had lost. Then he lifted Michelle's hand and gently placed something under it.

The atmosphere was tense that day. Linda couldn't withhold her anger toward Jason any longer. At one point she said

"We're going to get you!" to Jason. Linda spoke openly with guests about her belief that Jason murdered Michelle. A cemetery worker told Pat Young that she'd overheard Linda telling Meredith that they should just take Cassidy and run. This was concerning and would result in a lot of conflict between the two families in the coming months.

Meredith spoke to some of Michelle's friends from college. Oddly, she mentioned her plan to lose enough weight to fit into Michelle's clothes. She would later ask Jason to retrieve Michelle's clothes for her after police released the house.

Meredith asked Michelle's friends if they believed Jason was responsible for Michelle's death. When they responded no, she didn't have any more to do with them. It made an already difficult day that much worse for everyone. Why all the immediate accusations? Jason had never given Michelle's family any reason to believe he would harm her.

Jason ended up telling Alan to bring June with him on the trip for support, but that it would be best for her not to attend the funeral, so that's what he did. Linda and Meredith didn't even reserve a seat for Alan. Jason's sister, Kim gave up her seat for him.

Jason and his mother moved to an extended-stay hotel for another week while they were waiting to (hopefully) get the Explorer and their other belongings back from police. Cassidy was taken to Brevard with Joe and Heather to shield her from the drama and the ever persistent media.

CHAPTER 4

Crime scene observations

Investigators searched the house for approximately two weeks before releasing it back to Jason. They collected a great deal of items from the house and even went through all the kitchen drawers and made copies of every document, note and card. They did the same with the side table drawers in the master bedroom. It appeared they were very thorough, yet they actually missed a lot of things. Jason's sister, Kim was the first person to enter the home after it was released and her observations prompted her to bring in a private investigator to look things over. She hired Dr. Maurice Godwin at that time. Together, they identified several items that were left behind by investigators.

The murder weapon was not found and the object has never been identified, but there are some indications that it may have been an iron. There were pointed blood swipes on the sheet [iv]that appeared to have possibly been left by an iron. They didn't appear to be knife swipes and Michelle did not appear to have been stabbed. Kim did not find the iron in the home after police released the house, and police did not collect an iron into evidence. Dr. Godwin took the following photos of the iron-like blood smears.

Images taken by Dr. Godwin

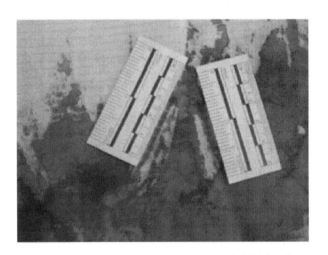

Michelle's side of the bed (left side) was covered in blood. Some Progress Energy paperwork was found on the side table bed, so it's possible she was reviewing it before going to sleep. There was also a very large puddle of blood near the closet door, not far from where the body was found. There was so much that it leaked into the ceiling below. There was blood spattered on the wall and an indication that the killer would have at one point lifted Michelle's head to get into Jason's closet. What was in the closet? Both Jason's and Michelle's closets appeared to have been rummaged through. In fact, all of the closets in the upstairs rooms were in disarray.

Special Agent Duane Deaver of the State Bureau of Investigation believed that it would have taken a long time for Michelle to die—possibly an hour or more. She would have been incapacitated long before she'd died, so if it was a robbery, they would have been able to easily collect what they came for and left. Someone wanted her dead.

There were pillows all around Michelle's body and one between her legs. First responders had to move the pillows to get to the body. Two of the pillows had clear and distinctly different foot impressions—evidence that two people were involved in the killing. One of the prints showed a "10" in a small circle, indicating the size of the shoe. Jason wore a size 12, so it wasn't his footprint.

Two drawers from Michelle's large wooden jewelry box on the dresser were missing. Michelle's wedding and engagement rings had been removed from her hand. Jason had a second platinum wedding ring that was missing from the box where it was normally stored in the master bathroom. Jason's wallet with five-hundred dollars in cash was missing. Costume jewelry was left behind—only the valuable pieces were taken. Engraved jewelry was also left behind.

There were child-sized bloody footprints in the hall bathroom, but no trail of footprints—indicating that Cassidy would have been picked up and carried to the bathroom multiple times. There were also bloody foot-prints on the step-stool against the sink.

There was a pair of Cassidy's balled-up bloody socks under her yellow duck robe in the bathroom. Investigators failed to document or collect them. They were very saturated with blood. There was another bloody sock in the hallway. As mentioned previously, this was an important clue because Cassidy was unable to put socks on by herself.

Photo provided by Dr. Godwin

Down the hall in Cassidy's bedroom, the music player had been left on. It was unusual because the Youngs hadn't used it to help her fall sleep since she was an infant. There was no blood found in her room, but her closet door was open. An empty plastic comforter bag was found on the floor. It seemed obvious that someone was searching for something in that house, but what?

Downstairs in the kitchen, there was a small metal trash can on top of the counter. Michelle was very organized and kept the house neat and tidy, so this was unusual—it appeared to be evidence of a clean-up. There was a small smear of blood on the kitchen cabinet beneath the sink and a speck of blood which was later identified as Michelle's on the doorknob the led into the garage.

The hose behind the house was lying on the sidewalk and there was a slow trickle of water. There was no sign of forced entry, so Wake County Sheriff Donnie Harrison declared that it was not a random crime and that neighbors had nothing to fear. Was it too early to make that statement? After all, the garage door was broken . . . the door leading into the house was never locked. How difficult would it be for someone to enter the home?

***

Jason and Michelle had a gentle black lab-mix named Mr. Garrison. They called him "Mr. G." They had the fenced back yard for him to run around in, but he normally slept in his dog bed at night, in the corner of the master bedroom. He always stayed indoors when they weren't home. Mr. G. was very friendly and rarely barked—the perfect family dog.

When Meredith went to the house on Friday afternoon, she reported that the fence was open, yet the gate was closed in crime scene photos. The gate at the opposite end of the house was in fact open though. Meredith told police that the dog was freaking out when she was attempting to enter the home through the front door. She claimed that she saw bloody paw prints throughout the house . . . yet investigators didn't find a single paw print or any sign that the dog had been roaming freely in the house. How is that possible? If he was inside for fourteen hours, surely he would have gotten into the blood. There was an enormous amount of blood in the master bedroom and blood in the hall bathroom. At the end of the 911 call, Meredith said "Come on, buddy" to get the dog to head outside with her and Cassidy. This was confirmation that the dog was inside the house, but then how does one explain the absence of bloody paw prints? Oddly, Meredith didn't secure Mr. G. in the fenced back yard, so he was left wandering around outside.

Fifteen year old Kyle Gilgen lived next door to the Youngs. When he went out to get the mail that afternoon, he noticed Mr. G. wandering loose. He told police he would secure the dog at his house. Later that evening, Jason's brother-in-law, Stephen went by the house to try to find the dog for Jason, and thankfully he was safe with the Gilgens. Stephen and Kim looked him over carefully and he had no blood on his paws or anywhere on his body. They took the dog to Jason, who was still staying at Meredith's at the time. Meredith became hysterical. She was worried that the dog would be covered in blood. Kim assured her that the dog was clean and she finally calmed down.

***

As mentioned, investigators missed a lot of things. Since police still hadn't released the cause of death, Kim was trying to determine what had happened to Michelle. She found a tooth in the master bedroom near the baseboard. She collected the item and that was when she decided to seek outside assistance to see if anything else had been overlooked. Dr. Godwin found a hair in a picture frame which was sitting on the dresser near the body. He found other items of possible relevance. There was a child's yellow robe on the bathroom floor with what appeared to be a bloody finger-print. He found and collected the bloody socks from the hall bathroom. He collected and photographed the sheets with the iron-like impressions. He also noticed that the bathroom with the bloody footprints hadn't been dusted for fingerprints, nor had other areas of the house. He collected several bags of items and took a lot of photos. The items were turned over to investigators a short time later.

Kim found used diapers in the trash can that were folded a different way than what was typical for Michelle and Jason. They would roll the diapers up and then tape them with the diaper tape. There were two diapers that were not folded at all. This is important because Cassidy was found without a diaper. Normally, she would remove her pants and diaper and wait for someone to dress her. That day, she was found in her pants, diaper removed. It was an indication that someone was caring for her. It did not appear that she'd been left alone all night and into the following day. Police believed that only someone who loved the child would take the time to clean her up. They believed that person was Jason, even though it didn't make sense because so much time would have lapsed by the time the body was discovered. Investigators missed these important clues—the used diapers, the bloody socks, the bathrobe, the sheets, and more.

On another occasion, Kim and her husband Gary went back to the house to continue cleaning and packing it up in anticipation of listing it for sale. The locks had recently been changed because Meredith still had a house key and they didn't want anyone in the house. And really, she shouldn't have had any need to enter the house. Plus she'd made the strange comments just after Michelle was found and they didn't know exactly what they were dealing with at that time.

Linda and Meredith showed up that day and demanded to be let into the house. Kim and Stephen refused, at which time the Fishers spent the next forty-five minutes yelling and banging on the doors and windows all around the house. After they'd had enough of that, Kim and Stephen attempted to leave in their truck, but the Fishers' car was blocking them. Linda and Meredith began beating on the truck. Stephen told them to move their car, or he was going to run it over and they finally complied. What possible reason did the Fishers' have to react so violently? Why did they need to get into the house?

***

Crime scenes in Wake County are processed by an agency known as C.C.B.I. — City County Bureau of Investigations. They are responsible for collecting items for forensic testing such as blood, DNA and fingerprints. After looking at this case and another questionable case from this same county, it's clear that there is a disadvantage to having a separate agency process the scene. How do they determine which items are important in identifying the killer(s)? In this particular case, it was critical to determine if the child was truly left alone. That would enable the detectives to narrow down the list of suspects, but C.C.B.I. missed this key point. They didn't collect the bloody socks; they didn't swab the (possibly staged) bathroom for prints or search the drains in that bathroom for signs of blood, and they left behind a lot of items that could have possibly identified the killers.

Michelle's purse wasn't processed for prints or DNA, even though it was tipped over on the floor. Though they swabbed the jewelry box for DNA testing, they didn't collect this key piece of evidence. The 911 call was very odd, yet police didn't collect the clothing Meredith had been wearing to search for evidence of blood. An absence of blood would have been incriminating. It would have been an indication that she hadn't actually checked on her sister that day as she'd claimed. It would have pointed toward her possible knowledge of Michelle's death at the time the 911 call was placed, but unfortunately police didn't investigate the possibility.

CHAPTER 5

Alibis

Naturally the spouse is always a suspect in a murder case. Statistics <u>indicate</u> that at least a third of spousal murders against women are committed by the husband, so police immediately began investigating Jason. His failure to speak to them likely added to their suspicion. They needed to determine where he was that night. Who was he communicating with? Did he have an alibi? Was there motive? There were lots of questions and they needed to figure it out without his assistance.

Within a day of the murder, police discovered that Jason had spent the night of November 2 at the Hampton Inn in Hillsville, Virginia. Officers were sent to speak to the hotel staff. They needed to determine his arrival and departure time and whether anything unusual occurred during his stay. They confirmed that he checked in at 10:54 p.m. and that his key card had only been swiped one time, just after check-in. They also determined that he was on his computer until 11:53 p.m. This really strained the timeline when considering Jason's possible involvement. He would have had to drive the approximately three hour drive back to Raleigh, placing him there at approximately 3:00 a.m., then committed the murder and made the long trip back to the hotel. Was it even possible? It was very tight.

Jason would have had to function with no sleep the entire next day—which consisted of lots of driving and visits with customers. Did it make sense? Could he have done this? His hotel receipt and a copy of USA Today with the affixed Hampton Inn sticker were found in his Explorer. His cell phone pinged on a tower in Wytheville at 7:40 a.m., so everything seemed to indicate that he had spent the night in Hillsville, and left the hotel by seven that morning. Still, they wondered if he could have somehow pulled this off. They even checked to see if he had chartered a flight. He hadn't.

Further stretching the already tight timeline, the State Bureau of Investigations had determined that it took Michelle a long time to die, possibly an hour or more. He would have also needed time to clean up afterward . . . and then there's Cassidy. Someone cleaned her up too. Would she have remained clean for ten-plus hours? The timeline seemed impossible, yet police held onto the belief that he had somehow managed to kill his wife. Jason didn't have a scratch on his body and no blood was found in his Explorer or his hotel room. Plus there were two sets of footprints at the crime scene, indicating two people murdered Michelle.

What about Meredith? She discovered the body and placed the 911 call. She was also out within the time-of-death window in the early morning hours of November 3, yet investigators didn't consider her possible involvement. For example, rather than transferring her car to the crime lab garage as they did with Jason's Explorer, Detective David merely looked inside and determined that "nothing related to the crime" was found in the vehicle, therefore it was never forensically examined for blood or DNA.

Investigators knew there were issues with Meredith's story. They knew there were no dog prints in the house, even though Meredith claimed he was there when she'd arrived. There wasn't blood "all over the house" as she had stated during the 911 call. They had to find it odd that she didn't turn her sister's body over to attempt CPR. Her car keys were found on her sister's Lexus. She made strange statements to Jason's family. Why weren't they investigating her? Is it because she was "cooperating" with police?

What about her timeline the night of the murder? Records indicated that she called Colleen at 2:27 a.m. Surveillance cameras confirm she arrived at Sheetz at 3:36 a.m. and was seen standing in line inside the store, then exited and drove off at 3:56 a.m. Meredith used her cell phone to check her bank account balance at 4:17 a.m. That was the last phone activity until Jason called and left her the message about picking up the print-outs. It's clear that Meredith had an unverifiable alibi for a good part of the night and into the morning of November 3.

Meredith gave police the name of the bartender she claimed had served them that night, but the bartender was unable to verify that Meredith and Betsy were there. She did not know them or remember them. Police did not make further attempts to verify that Meredith had been at the Carolina Ale House that night. They did not request receipts or inquire about possible surveillance videos to prove she was there. They focused all of their efforts on Jason. Meredith was simply a loose end with some questionable behaviors, but police ignored them.

CHAPTER 6

Neighborhood witnesses

Cindy Beaver, a resident of the Enchanted Oaks neighborhood was heading to work the morning of November 3 at around 5:30 – 5:35. She is certain of the time, because she'd worked at the post office for sixteen years and maintained a regular schedule to begin her six o'clock shift. She reported seeing a light colored SUV at the base of the Young's driveway with its headlights on, as if ready to pull out onto the road. She saw two people inside—a thin white male with his hands on the steering wheel and a heavy-set white female with dark frizzy hair in the passenger seat. She noticed the woman turned her head toward the driver and appeared to be talking to him. Interestingly, the woman matched the description of Meredith Fisher, but police seemed to ignore that detail.

Cindy also recalled that the driveway pillar lights were on, as well as many of the house lights, both inside and out. She saw a white van that she believed to be the newspaper delivery truck parked on a side street just past the Young's home. A man was inside with the interior light on and appeared to be sorting through papers. It is unclear whether it was a newspaper delivery truck or someone involved in the murder, since he was there at the same time as the light SUV.

Initially police were asking the public to report anything suspicious between midnight and *5 o'clock* that morning. Cindy assumed that her observations were unrelated since she saw the vehicles after that time, but police soon extended the time to six o'clock. After mentioning what she saw to her boss, he actually called police on her behalf. Since he was formerly a law enforcement officer, he felt it was important to report it.

Police interviewed Cindy four days after the murder, when the information was still fresh in her mind. She told them exactly what she saw. They interviewed her several times after that and at some point they actually attempted to discredit her story and confuse her about the date. This witness was a problem for them because Jason couldn't have been sitting in the driveway that late. He would have never made it back to the hotel by seven. This was a clear sign of tunnel vision. Police were attempting to ignore the disconfirming facts.

Terry Tiller, a newspaper delivery woman, noticed that the Young house was brightly lit between four and five o'clock that morning. The pillar, front doorway, and interior lights drew her attention to a house that she typically didn't notice since the house was normally dark at that time of the morning. She also noticed a light colored SUV, but couldn't recall exactly where she saw it. She believed it was up near the house, but not in the driveway, and it appeared to be positioned as if someone was loading things into the vehicle. She did not see any drivers in the vehicle.

A third witness also described seeing a light colored SUV that morning. Faye Hensley had a regular hair appointment every Friday. She was heading to the beauty salon at approximately seven-thirty and noticed a vehicle parked at the end of the Young's driveway near the mailbox. She described the color as gun metal gray. There may have been someone in the driver's seat but she couldn't be certain. There was no one in the passenger seat.

Remember that Jason was near Wytheville, Virginia at seven-forty that morning and it was verified that he had his hotel receipt and his newspaper from the Hampton Inn in Hillsville. The witness' sightings should have prompted investigators to consider other suspects, but instead they believed that the SUV occupants must have been Jason's accomplices, even though they never found any evidence that he'd been conspiring with someone.

Police didn't seem to consider that the bushy-haired woman described by Cindy Beaver may have been Meredith. They never showed Cindy a photo line-up that included Meredith's photo. How could they ignore something like that?

Although Michelle's SUV matched the description described by all three witnesses, none of them were shown photos of the Lexus, which may have been driven by the murderers. Tunnel vision seemed to be influencing their objectiveness.

CHAPTER 7

Jason's relationships

Pseudonyms will be used to shield the identity of some of the witnesses.

Beginning the very afternoon that Michelle was found, investigators with the Wake County Sheriff's Office began looking into every aspect of Jason Young's life—his daily habits, phone usage, the state of his marriage, past relationships, possible affairs and his financial status. They looked closely at all of his friends and family members hoping they would find evidence that one of them assisted in the crime. Since there were two sets of footprints, they believed there must have been an accomplice. Cindy Beaver's sighting of two people in an SUV also supported the theory that two people were involved in the murder.

Instead of remaining open to all possibilities, investigators focused on finding evidence of Jason's involvement and identifying his accomplice(s). There was never a consideration that Meredith may have had an accomplice, even though a witness described a person matching her description at the scene the morning of the murder. They believed Jason was the killer, so the disconfirming information was ignored.

Jason had a stable upbringing and supportive family who loved Michelle, so it was foolish for police to seriously consider that he'd relied on his mother or sisters to help him murder Michelle, yet they investigated them as such and naturally came up empty.

Police put the heat on all of his friends as well, even though they were stable relationships. These were people that he'd known for years who also loved Michelle. Most of the Young's friends were couples with small children like themselves. How logical would it be for one of them to risk everything to help him murder his wife . . . and for what? There was no evidence that any large payout had occurred. Yet they became a focus of the investigation with multiple lengthy interviews that went on for years and turned up nothing, aside from details about Jason's immaturity and obnoxiousness when he drank.

Police did however notice that Jason had a lot of phone communication with a woman in Florida named Molly Crawford*over the past few months, to include the time leading up to the murder. It turns out that she was one of Michelle's sorority sisters from NC State. Many of the women remained in touch after college and would continue getting together a few times a year. Often spouses and children were included. In July 2006, they all met up in Myrtle Beach at one of the sorority sister's homes. On that particular trip, Molly broke down about some marital problems she was experiencing. Jason and one of Molly's female friends were present at the time.

In September the same group got together for a long weekend at the Youngs'. They would all attend a NC State football game together. Molly and her husband, Greg stayed with the Youngs for four nights. Jason and Molly had an opportunity to talk privately that weekend and he asked her how her marriage was doing. Molly told him that it still wasn't great. They realized how much they enjoyed talking with each other and from that time on they began communicating with each other daily.

Since Molly lived in another state, she and Jason didn't physically see each other, but the two of them became very close, and soon realized that they wanted the relationship to progress beyond friendship. One weekend in October when Molly's husband was away, Jason traveled to Florida to see her. They were intimate that weekend and neither of them wanted Monday to arrive, though both agreed that the relationship was wrong and that it couldn't go anywhere. Neither of them had plans to leave their spouses. They both wanted their marriages to work, yet they weren't ready to break communication with each other. They continued speaking to each other daily up to and including the time of Michelle's death.

Molly learned of Michelle's death the evening of November 3 from the sorority sister who had hosted the get-together that summer. Shocked and devastated at the news, she booked the first available flight to Raleigh, which was scheduled for early the next morning. There she met up with her husband who had been out of town, and a few other friends, and they all went to Meredith's to offer support for Jason and Cassidy. There wasn't much talking. Everyone was in shock over Michelle's death and didn't even know what to say, but it meant a lot to Jason that they were there for him.

Molly attended the funeral and then she and her husband returned to Florida the following day. That is when her personal nightmare began. As soon as her name was mentioned in the public search warrants, the media began hounding her. They wanted to know everything about Molly. She was the equivalent of Amber Frey and they wouldn't leave her alone. They contacted all of her friends and family to try to learn more about her. She avoided everyone. She didn't want to speak to the media or have her picture plastered all over the news. She rarely left the house. Throughout this time, she was not in contact with Jason at all.

The media harassment was only part of her nightmare. Police wouldn't leave her alone either. They would show up at her door at all hours of the day and night. They visited multiple times to question her. They asked her about her relationship with Jason and tried to determine if she'd had any involvement in Michelle's death. At one point she had girlfriends in town for a spa weekend as they were all turning thirty that year. Sadly, Michelle was to be included in the event. Police wanted to fingerprint everyone who was present. Molly and her husband went to the police station first, while friends looked after their son. At that point police informed her husband about the affair, not even allowing her the opportunity to tell him herself. They were really putting the pressure on her.

Weeks later police obtained a search warrant to retrieve her laptop and search her home. Molly felt isolated and traumatized from the intrusions into her personal life. Thus far, police were unable to find anything connecting Molly or her husband to Michelle's death, but the harassment continued. Police wanted someone to break. They felt confident that if they continued pressuring his family and friends, sooner or later the truth would come out and the case would be solved.

***

Amanda Thompson*, a childhood friend of Jason's would also have her world turned upside down by investigators. Amanda visited the Raleigh area for a real estate course at the end of October 2006. She knew Jason from a camp she'd attended every summer from the age of six on into her teens. Jason had been an instructor and was a few years older than Amanda, but they became friends and stayed in touch into adulthood. They talked to each other every few months or so and saw each other when Amanda visited the area, which wasn't often. She was married and had built a life in Montana.

Amanda stayed with the Youngs while attending the classes. Jason picked her up from the airport and drove her to her class each morning. She had an opportunity to meet Cassidy but didn't meet Michelle until a couple of days later since she was in New York when Amanda arrived in town. Amanda had spoken to Michelle many times by phone but they had never met in person. When Michelle arrived home they all had dinner together. Michelle showed Amanda the new baby's room and some of the new, adorable outfits she had picked out for him. The baby would be named Rylan.

That evening Jason asked to see Amanda's wedding rings. He was goofing around and pretended to swallow her rings. He told her she would have to wait until the next day to give them back . . . after they'd passed. Of course Jason was teasing her all along and hadn't really swallowed them. He returned the rings to her the next morning. However, Michelle told others about the incident, and after her death Meredith shared the story with police. This highlighted Jason's immaturity of course, but did it in any way indicate that he was capable of murder? This incident was typical of Jason. He was still very much like a kid, but that's one of the things that made him such a good father. He knew how to have fun with Cassidy and the connection between the two was obvious to friends and family.

Amanda confirmed the story with police, but so what? Were they really making progress with the investigation? They were unable to find any evidence that Amanda was involved in

Michelle's death. They verified her flight information and knew that she was not in Raleigh at the time of the murder, but they continued digging into her private life. It seemed they'd decided to use her to attack Jason's character. This typically happens when police are unable to find evidence of their prime suspects' involvement.

CHAPTER 8

2007

The investigation had been underway for four months by the spring of 2007. Police believed they had made some progress, but certainly didn't have enough proof to make any arrests. They continued to remain focused on Jason and all of his associates—family members, old girlfriends, friends, co-workers and people he went to school with. They had yet to identify a conspirator or anything unusual, such as large money transfers after the murder. Police made some changes and new investigators were assigned to the case. Detective Richard Spivey would replace Detective Brent David as lead investigator moving forward. Detective Blackwell also took on more of a role in the investigation.

Meredith had grown to trust Detective David. They spoke frequently and there was never any suspicions raised about her possible involvement, so she was disappointed with the leadership change. The new detectives were beginning to question her more intently. Meredith reiterated the same points about that night in each interview. She told police that Michelle wouldn't have slept in the clothing she was found in—the hooded sweatshirt in particular. She also stressed the fact that Michelle couldn't see without her contacts and would typically remove them and then wear her eyeglasses at night. She asked police if they found her glasses near the bed. They had not. It's unclear why she was fixated on rather trivial details.

Meredith offered no explanations for the illogical things—such as the absence of dog prints in the house, or her car keys oddly found on the hood of the Lexus. Plus the inconsistencies in her story continued to mount. In a previous interview with Detective David, she stated that she did not know Shelly was at the house that night, but she told the new detectives that Michelle informed her the day before that Shelly would be there. When asked how Cassidy got to the bathroom since there was no trail of footprints, she suggested that someone either picked her up, or Cassidy crawled. Was this the first time she was asked to explain this? Instead of stating that she'd "tried a key to the front door but it didn't work", she said that she realized right away that when she approached the front door that she did not have the Young's house key with her.

As a side note, the house key story is interesting because Meredith had been by the house on October 22—two weeks prior to Michelle's death. Amanda was in town that day and she and Jason were just leaving, but spoke for a few minutes. Jason actually told Meredith his idea about buying Michelle the purse that day. Meredith had to enter the house that day too, but didn't approach the front door, or attempt to enter the back garage door. She lifted the broken garage door and walked right in. Why then did she create a story about all the various ways she'd attempted to enter the home the day Michelle was found? Add it to the list of suspicions.

Meredith was asked a little about Colleen's background. The highlight of the questioning was the fact that Colleen had trouble paying her bills on time. Detective Blackwell's hand written notes from the interview:

> Has bill problems. Bill collectors stopped calling around October.

It's certainly interesting that the bill collectors stopped calling just before Michelle's death. Again, did this raise a red flag?

As the police investigation progressed, so did the tension between the families. Right after the funeral, Jason and Cassidy moved in with Heather and Joe who lived close to Brevard. The decision to move was based partially on the way Linda and Meredith behaved at the funeral, but there was also a desire to shield Cassidy from the media. Since this was a national news story, the media was everywhere. It was best to leave town. A few months later, Jason and Cassidy moved in with Pat and Gerald in Brevard.

The move made it difficult for Meredith and Linda to see Cassidy, but it was their own doing for being so vocal at the funeral. Logically, Jason didn't want his daughter around people who were accusing him of harming her mother. There had also been rumor that Meredith and Linda had discussed kidnapping Cassidy. Jason felt it was prudent to limit and also supervise the visits, so he made sure family or friends were always present. They could visit once a month or so.

The visits usually lasted two to three hours and they would sometimes arrange to meet at a half-way point. For example on one occasion they met in Charlotte at one of Jason's friend's homes. After each visit, Meredith and Linda (if she was present) would go to the police to share their observations. Police were very interested in the feedback because Jason still wasn't talking to them, at his attorney's advisement.

Over the next couple of months the new investigative team took a closer look at Meredith and particularly her alibi. They needed to speak to those she'd had contact with that night. In May, 2007 Colleen was interviewed again and there were some inconsistencies from her initial interviews that had taken place just after the murder. She initially stated that Meredith arrived home at around two a.m., but this time she said she heard the garage door at three a.m. By this point, she likely knew that she couldn't have heard Meredith arrive home at two because Meredith called her at 2:27 a.m.

Colleen was asked what Cassidy was wearing when she arrived at the Birchleaf home, and she stated that she was wearing pink pajamas, no socks and no coat and that she *was* wearing a diaper. She said Cassidy had a teddy bear, which was odd because Meredith said she didn't grab anything for her before leaving the house. In earlier interviews, Colleen stated that Cassidy was wearing socks and no diaper and there was no mention of a teddy bear.

Colleen stated that the fire truck had not yet arrived at the Birchleaf home when she got there, but how could that be possible? Meredith said the fire truck was pulling up near the end of the 911 call. That would have been before she'd even called Colleen to ask her to come to the house.

Police asked Colleen to provide more specifics about Meredith's odd comments the evening that Michelle was found. She recalled Meredith telling the Young family how she initially thought the whole thing was a joke, but then realized it wasn't when she saw Michelle lying on her stomach. She told them there were bloody dog and child footprints in the bedroom (there weren't). She said that she believed Cassidy's step stool was against the sink because she was looking for band-aids for Michelle. Remember that Meredith also told Pat Young that

Michelle had band-aids all over her. After the murder, Jason's sister Kim asked Cassidy to open a band-aid for her and Cassidy was unable to open it. Was the band-aid story fabricated to make it appear the child was alone all night . . . searching for band-aids to help her mother—the bloody step-stool evidence of such? Was it part of a staged crime scene? No band-aids or wrappers were found.

Colleen was asked if she heard Meredith crank up the lawn mower that day. Colleen responded that Meredith had told her she had been unable to start the mower. That is inconsistent with what Meredith initially told police. She did not say she couldn't start it, only that she had difficulty with the mulch. Colleen confirmed that the keys on Michelle's Lexus hood belonged to Meredith. *How* did her keys end up there? After the interview, Colleen failed a polygraph examination. She was very upset, so weeks later investigators agreed to conduct a second examination, but she failed that one too. Investigators didn't seem too concerned about it.

***

The Fishers' visits with Cassidy continued over the next few months, but they were unhappy with the constant supervision. They continued to provide police with summaries of the visits. Meredith began using it as an opportunity to cast suspicion on Jason, in a likely attempt to keep suspicion away from her. After one particular visit, she described how Cassidy would begin a sentence about her mother and then stop mid-sentence for no apparent reason. She also told police that they played hide and seek and Cassidy went to hide with Meredith and told her she had a secret, but she never revealed it. Was Meredith implying that Cassidy's "secret" was that Jason killed Michelle? It is ridiculous to believe that a three year old child communicates that way. Of course the band-aid story was equally silly, but it was Meredith's way of adding drama to the tragedy . . . the poor child was alone and trying to help her mother by applying band-aids to her dead body—only it wasn't true and police knew it.

Jeanne Dulworth, a social worker friend of Jason's, supervised some of the visits. She had known Jason since childhood and firmly believed in his innocence. She agreed to meet with police to share her observations from the visits. She thought some of the Fishers' behaviors were odd. On one occasion when they'd met at a hotel, Meredith said to Cassidy "Let's run to the room." They arrived at the hotel room before Jeanne could get there and they opened the door, went inside and tried to close it, but she got there in time to prevent the door from closing. The Youngs were very protective of Cassidy in light of the comments made by Linda about taking Cassidy and fleeing.

Jeanne went on to describe a subsequent visit the Fishers had with Cassidy at Pat Young's home. Jeanne told police that the Fishers locked Cassidy's bedroom door with Cassidy in the room with them. They also took a Barbie doll and laid it face down and told Cassidy, "Look, it's Sleeping Beauty." Cassidy didn't like that and she immediately took the Barbie and stood it up. That was an unusual thing to do considering how the doll was found next to her mother's dead body. Interestingly, Cassidy had told her Aunt Kim that "Mommy was Sleeping Beauty", so it's interesting that the Fishers referenced the doll that way. Did Cassidy obtain the Sleeping Beauty reference from Meredith?

Linda shared a completely different version of the doll play with police. She told them that *Cassidy* laid the Barbie doll face-down next to the bed of her doll house and said "Mommy's dead."

Were the Fishers trying to reinforce to police that Cassidy had seen her mother dead?

Jeanne also told police that a heated argument occurred when she informed Meredith that she had advised Jason not to allow the visits until the murder was solved. At that point Meredith started to cry and said that she had asked Jason to bring Cassidy and move in with her. Jeanne asked her how she could do that if she believed he had killed Michelle. Meredith replied that she was ninety percent certain he did not kill Michelle, but she wanted to ask him some questions. Jeanne asked Meredith if she felt that strongly about his innocence; why not inform the media of that? She did not respond.

Finally, Jeanne wanted police to know some of the comments Meredith had made. She stated that Cassidy had been taken away from her, that she had lost her mother and taking her away meant the two most important people in her life were gone. Jeanne asked, "What about Jason?" and Meredith said, "Oh yes, he is important too." Jeanne told police that Meredith also said. "You don't know what Cassidy and I had to watch." Why would she make a comment like that unless she had been there?

The Fishers' visits with Cassidy came to a halt over a confrontation about a news article. The article stated that the Fishers were complaining because Jason wasn't allowing them to see Cassidy, and it simply wasn't true. Pat wanted them to arrange for a retraction. Things escalated and Linda got very upset and started yelling. Jason decided that it was time to put a stop to the visits. He didn't want Cassidy to be exposed to this. The Fishers were very upset over this and months went by with no visits . . . gifts to Cassidy were returned unopened.

***

With summer approaching and still little progress in the investigation, detectives must have believed it was wise to question Meredith more extensively, so they arranged for the S.B.I (State Bureau of Investigation) to speak to her. Agents interrogated Meredith about some of the inconsistencies in her story. She had stated during the 911 call that there was blood "all over the house", when in fact it was limited to the master bedroom and hall bathroom. She explained that she realized she had been mistaken when she did a walk-through with Detective David right after the murder. The "blood all over the house" statement seemed to indicate that there was blood all over the house at some point but a clean-up had taken place. In fact, small specks of blood *were* found on the kitchen cabinet and door knob, so is it possible that Meredith did see blood "all over" the house?

The SBI agents informed Meredith that a witness described an SUV with a woman matching her description at the house that morning.

> Fisher was advised that a car was seen early that morning with a person who looked like her in it. She replied that it did not make sense and why would she *go back* over to the house if she did it. [v]

That statement seemed to indicate that she had been at the house earlier. Next, she discussed the fact that she was in bed "when it happened."

> She knew she was innocent because she was in bed when it happened.

Well, she didn't go to bed until after four that morning, so how could she be so sure that the murder occurred after 4:15? Interestingly, that is near the time when the witnesses saw the light SUV at the house.

Meredith explained that she understood why she looked like a suspect.

> She said she understood why she looked like a suspect. She was close to Michelle at the Sheetz gas station when it happened, while he was far away in Virginia.

Could that statement indicate that Meredith intentionally went to the Sheetz store to create an alibi? Also, could it indicate that she knew Michelle was being killed at the time she was at Sheetz? How else could she say that she was at the Sheetz gas station *when it happened*?

The interview ended without a confession from Meredith, but did investigators realize how incriminating her statements were? What would happen next?

Colleen was interviewed by the detectives again the next day. There were inconsistencies from her May interview. This time Cassidy didn't have a teddy bear, she had a doll. She also stated that Cassidy had on at least one sock. She said that Meredith had to take Cassidy into the bathroom at Target to put a diaper on her and change her clothing. In her prior interview, she remembered that Cassidy was wearing a diaper that day. Meredith insists Cassidy was not wearing a diaper when she found her.

When Colleen was asked about Meredith's possible involvement, she said "My brain says Jason is going to or did use Meredith and that she is going to be the number one suspect." She also said "Meredith is more level headed than I am—she can stay more calm than I can in stressful situations."

***

Next, police focused on Meredith's drinking buddy, Betsy Browning. Betsy said that she and Meredith were co-workers at Lucky 32, and quickly became close friends. In fact, at the time of the interview she was living with Colleen and Meredith in the Fuquay-Varina home.

When asked about the night of the murder, Betsy told police that she was already at the Carolina Ale House when Meredith arrived. Police asked Betsy what Meredith was wearing that night and she remembered that Meredith was wearing her work clothes—black pants, white button-up shirt, and black shoes. Incidentally, police never asked Meredith to provide those black shoes to compare them to the bloody shoe prints at the crime scene.

Betsy said they remained at the Ale House until the bar closed at about 2:15 a.m. and then sat in the parking lot for ten minutes. Since Meredith had consumed several drinks, Betsy invited her to stay at her house so she wouldn't have to drive as far, but Meredith said she could always go to Michelle's if she felt it wasn't safe to drive all the way home. According to Betsy, they left separately at that point.

Betsy was asked if Meredith ever discussed what she did after she left the Ale House that night. Betsy said that Meredith didn't talk about it except that she did say that she had a "feeling" about that night after she'd left.

When police asked Betsy if she had ever been to the Young's house, she said "no," but later during the same interview she changed her statement and said she was there once before, but only on the front porch.

Police asked Betsy if she was aware of Meredith's and Colleen's interviews the prior week and she said she was. When they asked about their reactions to the interviews, Betsy stated that she'd overheard them talking about one of them lying and admitting to it. Police then told Betsy that Meredith was not truthful during the 911 call and admitted she had not really tried to roll Michelle over. Betsy didn't believe them, but they were being truthful. Meredith did in fact admit that she did not attempt to roll Michelle over.

Police met with Betsy's former room-mates to attempt to verify her alibi. She told police she was living with Michael and Laura Frank at the time of the murder. Police spoke to the couple in October, 2007. They were unable to alibi Betsy because they did not remember her coming home that night and did not remember seeing her car when they left to go to work that morning. They also recalled Betsy talking about the case and wondering, "Wow. We were all together that night and can't believe this happened."

Police decided it was time to get search warrants for Meredith's computer and home. They recognized that it was necessary and discussed exactly how the search warrant should be worded.

9-10-2007 email to Milar re: Blackwell request; scope of assistance:

> Hi Sarge, I'm just forwarding this request on through the chain of command for explicit instructions on what they wish done. I am anticipating the following activity that would relate to this request:

Scripting the search warrant, eyeballing Meredith Fisher's house like I would any other search warrant, conferring with Spivey and Blackwell on points of PC (probable cause I assume) relating to this subject and location. Reviewing report narratives for material usable as PC. I expect that <u>as long as our agency is going down this very serious road</u>, I would also ask for other items such as documents, journals, diaries, letters, greeting cards, receipts, photos, videos, bills, banking and financial statements, schooling records, psychology texts and notes from school, any books she may have on crime, mysteries, whodunits, and the like, whether they be in electronic or other physical form, Review of draft SW application(s) with you or other designated chain of command supervisor.[vi]

Oddly, the whole discussion suddenly dropped without explanation. There was no search warrant for Meredith's home. Police continued searching for evidence that tied Jason to the crime. It is unknown how the decision was made to forgo an investigation into Meredith's possible involvement, but that was the end of it. Detectives were forced to turn a blind eye to the numerous red flags.

CHAPTER 9

Convenience store witness

After verifying that Jason had checked into the Hampton Inn in Virginia the night of November 2, police explored the possibility that he'd somehow left unnoticed and traveled back to Raleigh to commit the murder. Maybe they could find a receipt to prove he hadn't remained in his hotel room, or find a witness who actually saw him near the time of the murder.

Detectives Ikerd and Broadwell reportedly began canvassing convenience stores and gas stations at midnight on November 4. They started at the hotel and traveled along the route Jason would have most likely taken had he returned to Raleigh. According to Ikerd's police narrative, they stopped at the Four Brothers store in King, North Carolina and spoke to a clerk named Gracie Bailey. When shown a picture of Jason, she allegedly told police that he looked like a man who was in her store the morning of November 2.

Detective Ikerd didn't take any notes during the interview. Detective Broadwell recorded one small notation on a hand-written *undated* list of stores in the area.

> Brothers Food Stores
> Gracie Bailey (was working) **No video**
> 106 Carmel Drive King, NC
> Tika Ingram (manager)
> pre-pay with cash, may have been there at 5 a.m.

Though it is standard practice for police to document interviews as quickly as possible to ensure that every detail is accurately captured, this particular interview was not summarized until *six months* later. One would expect an immediate follow-up in a situation such as this—a potential witness who could identify their number one suspect! Detective Ikerd wrote the following narrative in May, 2007.

> In the early morning hours of November 6, 2006, we stopped at a convenience store that was attached to a McDonald's restaurant in King, NC that was off Highway 52. We spoke with the clerk that was working that shift, Gracie Bailey, about the possibility of seeing Jason Young at the business in the early morning hours of November 3, 2006. Ms. Bailey was shown a "cropped" photograph only of Jason Young that was obtained from a photograph seized from the Young's residence on Birchleaf Drive.
>
> Ms. Bailey stated that she believes Jason Young had entered the store between 5:00 a.m. and 5:30 a.m. on November 3, 2006. She stated that she remembers him because she refused to turn the gas

pumps on while he was attempting to pump gas without him coming into the store first to pay for fuel. Ms. Bailey said that she remembers him being very agitated and said there was another "regular customer" in the store when he entered. Ms. Bailey stated that she and the other customer made a comment to each other after he exited the store about his temperament. Ms. Bailey said that she believed that this person was operating a white sport utility type vehicle.[vii]

Note all the additional details about the encounter. What began with a simple notation—"May have been there at 5 a.m." had evolved into a story about an angry customer.

Shortly after Ikerd wrote his report, Detectives Spivey and Blackwell interviewed Gracie again. She provided very specific details at that time. It is interesting that none of this information was obtained during the initial interview.

> Mrs. Bailey stated a white male with blondish hair, mid 20's to early 30's, wearing a shirt, no coat and what she believed to be blue jeans (but was not sure), entered the store cursing at her.

> Mrs. Bailey stated at nighttime, the gas pumps are prepaid and the white male cursed her and was extremely mad for having to come into the store to pay.

Mrs. Bailey stated she believed the white male gave her a $20 bill and got $15 worth of gas.

Mrs. Bailey was asked did she recall what type of vehicle the white male was driving and she stated a white SUV, which looked new to her. Mrs. Bailey stated she did not get the license plate off the SUV.

Mrs. Bailey stated <u>she thought she smelled alcohol on his breath</u>.

Since there were no surveillance cameras at the store, Jason would have a difficult time proving he *wasn't* there that morning, but there are several problems with the story. First, gas stations typically require cash paying customers to pre-pay before fueling, so why did this person expect anything different? Second, even if this person *had* been able to fuel up before paying, he still would have had to enter the store to pay after pumping the gas . . . so why become hot-headed about it as described by the clerk?

There was no way to avoid being seen inside the store. If this was Jason, how would he have known that this store didn't have cameras? And third, the person described by Gracie had the smell of alcohol on his breath. Surely Jason wouldn't have been drinking while making his way back to the hotel!

Investigators needed to determine whether this store would have been a logical stop for Jason. Consider Jason's fuel consumption. Police had his credit card statements and knew when and where he had purchased fuel.

Examination of gas mileage:

- Jason purchased a full tank of fuel in Raleigh before beginning the trip.
- He drove 84.8 miles to the Cracker Barrel restaurant, and another 83.9 miles to the Hampton Inn.
- The next morning, he drove 145 miles to Clintwood, Virginia. Since he got lost, twenty extra miles were added (~165 miles).
- He drove 46.6 miles to Duffield, Virginia and filled up the tank again. That adds up to 380.3 miles. 19.45 gallons of fuel was purchased = **19.55 miles/gallon.**
- Next, he traveled 137 miles to Transylvania Hospital, 5.8 miles to Brevard and 218 miles to Burlington where he stopped to fill up again. That adds up to 360.8 miles. 18.44 gallons of fuel was purchased = **19.5 miles/gallon**.

The gas mileage was consistent throughout his trip—very strong evidence that Jason did not drive back to Raleigh that night. If he had, the fuel consumption would have been off.

If one speculates that perhaps he purchased fuel with cash along the way to throw police off, they visited every store along that route and examined numerous surveillance videos. There was no sign that he had purchased gas with cash . . . aside from the alleged identification by Gracie. Does the stop at the 4 Brothers store even work?

Jason would have driven 170 miles back to Raleigh from the Hampton Inn—for a total of 340 miles since his fill-up at the onset of the trip. Its 121 miles from 5108

Birchleaf to the 4 Brothers store in King, North Carolina. That adds up to 461 miles. Even if he had driven back to Raleigh, committed the crime and began driving back to Virginia, he would have *run out of fuel* before reaching the 4 Brothers Store. Further, if he *had* purchased fifteen dollars worth of fuel in King, he would have run out before making it to his next stop for fuel in Duffield, Virginia. It just didn't work, and there was more.

Police allegedly collected the cash register roll from the 4 Brothers store a couple of days after the initial visit to the store. The problem is that the receipts in discovery are from **2007**. The murder occurred in **2006**. It is unclear if this is a document that police prepared for trial, or if this was provided by the store manager. The store is now closed, so it would be impossible to go back and verify the transactions from that morning. The $15 purchase is highlighted. (This author noticed the date issue while researching the case files).

11/3/2007	5:19	1-1486	Yes	Yes	10	10
11/3/2007	5:19	1-1487	No	Yes	0.63	
11/3/2007	5:26	1-1489	No	Yes	5.42	
11/3/2007	5:27	1-1490	Yes	Yes	15	15
11/3/2007	5:28	1-1491	No	Yes	2.13	
11/3/2007	5:28	1-1493	No	Yes	6.83	

Finally, the reliability of the witness is shaky at best. Gracie had a history of drug addiction and had also been collecting disability checks since childhood due to a traumatic brain injury from a car accident. Memory problems were naturally a concern . . . however, with so little evidence to work with, police would hold onto this witness. It's fairly easy to convince juries today that someone was at a certain location—*if* they have a witness who will positively identify them. It doesn't much matter if they can't identify the person with absolute certainty. Juries convict based on "could haves" all the time.

CHAPTER 10

Was the crime scene staged?

Examining a crime scene for possible staging is very important, but is often overlooked. Investigators didn't spend a lot of time considering the possibility of staging in this particular case, but maybe they should have.

Forensic Magazine published an interesting article about crime scene staging in the June 2016 issue. It was written by Vernon Geberth, a retired Lieutenant-Commander with the New York Police Department.

> Staging a scene occurs when the perpetrator purposely alters the crime scene to mislead the authorities and/or redirect the investigation. Staging is a conscious criminal action on the part of an offender to thwart an investigation.
>
> Crime scene staging events happen in all jurisdictions all across the United States, and seem to be increasing as people learn more about the processes of death investigations through the media, true crime books, television mystery shows, and movies. **In**

many staged crime scenes, the "staging" tends to be overdone, or is inconsistent with the events and initial statements.

Most offenders aren't familiar with the workings of a crime scene, or know differences between a burglary, rape, robbery, homicide, accident or suicide scene. They have an idea of how the scene may appear from television or the movies, and believe they can create those depictions. However, upon closer scrutiny by criminal investigators, along with the application of forensic techniques, the staging becomes readily apparent.[viii]

Of particular interest in this case are the bloody footprints in the hall bathroom. They were tiny, so it was obvious they were left by Cassidy. There were several things that weren't quite natural about the footprints.

They appeared to enter the bathroom, but not exit. None of the prints were facing toward the door.

They were all very bright. They didn't appear to fade in subsequent steps as one would naturally expect.

Many of the prints are just the ball of the foot, as if the child was held as they were made. As well, the steps do not appear to be natural. Notice the right footprint below. It is not a natural step. The heel is placed over top of the first footprint and there is a cluster of prints to the left with no heel prints.

There is no trail of blood from Michelle's body to the hall bathroom. Cassidy had to have been carried.

Progress Energy paperwork was found near Michelle's body. On one of the pages, there appeared to be a small bloody footprint with sock striations. After flipping through several sheets, investigators noticed a small bloody footprint with noticeable sock striations. It appeared as though the foot had been placed on the paper twice. Was this a "practice" impression for the staging of footprints in the bathroom?

As described above, staging may have occurred if things are inconsistent with the events or initial statements. Clearly, the presence and nature of these footprints are inconsistent with the events. Cassidy was clean. There was no trail of prints from the body to the bathroom. The prints all went in the same direction.

If the prints were staged—and it appears likely they were—that would indicate that someone wanted it to *appear* as if the child was left alone with the body. SBI Agent Duane Deaver noticed the prints and the fact that there were no foot prints in the area where blood was smeared on the wall. So, had Cassidy's feet already been cleaned by someone at that point? Two bloody socks were found on the bath mat in that very location.

> Transfer stains in bathroom (feet). A right foot stain heavier on ball and toes than in previous stains and no heel stain present. No left or right

feet, but the wall is covered in blood further inside.
ix

If the crime scene was staged to make it appear that Cassidy was alone, then Jason is innocent. The murderer and/or conspirator *would* have a need to stage the scene. Logically, if Jason cleaned Cassidy, how did she remain that way for ten or so hours before Meredith arrived at the home? Did the murderer/conspirator make a mistake by cleaning all the blood off Cassidy?

Investigators obtained a search warrant to search Michelle's Lexus SUV in July 2007. They specifically wanted to search for the presence of blood because of the way Cassidy was found. They were considering the possibility that Cassidy had been removed from the house.

> In addition to discovering the decedent, the decedent's child was reportedly discovered by Meredith Fisher as well. She said the 2 ½ year old child was discovered under the sheets of decedent's bed. Ms. Fisher has stated that the child was clean and her feet showed little to no signs of having walked through the blood that had pooled around her mother. The bed sheets on the side of the bed where the child was located showed no obvious sign of blood as well. This description is in contrast to the small bloodied footprints that were found on the floor of the child's bathroom.
>
> There was a small visible trace of what appears to be blood on the hallway carpet between the child's

bathroom and the decedent's bedroom. This would lead to a logical conclusion that the child had been carried from one room to the other in lieu of the amount of blood left on the bathroom floor. <u>In order to maintain the clean condition that the child was discovered, removal from the scene would have been the simplest action.</u>[x]

No blood was found in the Lexus, but the fact remains that if Jason committed the murder, there is no explanation for Cassidy's condition. If the state's theory is correct, and Jason drove all the way back to Raleigh that night from Virginia, what condition would one expect to find Cassidy in? She should have been covered in blood, frightened, hungry and tired, but Cassidy was fine. That is consistent with someone having cared for her in the hours she would have been alone.

Though no blood was visible on Cassidy's pajamas, the crime lab identified the presence of blood on the pajama pants and top. Blood had soaked through the fabric on a portion of the pants. It seems to indicate that the clothing may have been washed. That most certainly excludes Jason as he wouldn't have had time to do a load of laundry and make it back to the hotel in time to get ready for his meeting.

Also interesting is that according to Jason's sister, Kim, the Youngs had a child-proof door knob apparatus on Cassidy's door to secure her safely in her bedroom at night. Jason could have simply closed her door before committing the murder. She would have remained in there until someone arrived at the house. That would have been the most logical scenario, but police didn't seem to consider it. As the investigation progressed, the possibility that staging may have occurred was set aside. It didn't fit the theory that Jason murdered Michelle

CHAPTER 11

Timeline and phone calls

The timing of communication can be very important in an investigation. Investigators needed to carefully examine phone usage from the time that Michelle was known to still be alive and into the following several days. There could be important clues about when others were notified about her death. For example, if investigators determined that Linda Fisher booked her flight to Raleigh before the 911 call was made, it would be incriminating evidence of Meredith's involvement. Or if they found odd phone calls from Jason to an unknown person shortly before and/or after Michelle's death, it could indicate that a hit man had been hired.

Right off the bat, we can exclude Jason's phone usage as suspicious. He spoke to Molly several times, which actually reduces the likelihood of his involvement or knowledge of Michelle's death—who would be foolish enough to create a record of calls to a mistress around the time of a murder? There were also typical calls to his friends and his mother, Pat. The only thing investigators found to be unusual was the fact that his phone redialed Pat's number multiple times the day Michelle was found, but his calls kept dropping because he was driving in the mountains, so that explained the numerous call attempts.

The calls between Linda and Meredith are more interesting . . . and possibly suspicious. We already know that the 911 call was not placed from the home phone as Meredith had claimed. It is not on the phone record. If one wants to eliminate Meredith as a suspect, it is important to determine when exactly Linda Fisher received word of Michelle's death. The following are the calls between the two of them the afternoon of 11/3/06.

- Meredith retrieved Jason's message about picking up the print-outs at 12:14 p.m.
- Meredith called Linda at 12:46 p.m. (45 seconds)
- Linda called Meredith at 1:07 p.m. (5 minutes, 24 seconds)

Meredith told police she was pulling into Michelle's driveway as the call with her mother was ending, which would have been 1:13 p.m. This left twelve minutes between Linda's call and the 911 call, which occurred at 1:25. There is a timing problem then, because Meredith insisted that her walk through the house couldn't have taken longer than a minute and that she didn't clean anything up or thoroughly look around. She said she went straight for the house phone and dialed 911 when she discovered Michelle on the floor. What did she do during those twelve minutes? It doesn't make sense.

Is it possible that Meredith already knew Michelle was dead when she called Linda at 12:46? What if Linda called her back at 1:07 and was informed of Michelle's death at that time? They did speak for five minutes. Linda's interview with police on November 5, 2006 supports the possibility that she'd received the news before the 911 call was placed.

> Ms. Fisher stated that Meredith called her on 11-03-06 around 1:00-1:30 p.m. Ms. Fisher stated she believed Meredith called her from Michelle's house. Ms. Fisher stated she was at the beauty shop when Meredith first called.
>
> Ms. Fisher stated she believed Meredith had called her from inside Michelle's home. Ms. Fisher thought Meredith was using Michelle's house phone, but was not sure.
>
> Ms. Fisher stated she believed <u>she spoke to Meredith for about five minutes and was unsure if Meredith called 911 or her first</u>. Ms. Fisher stated Michelle was cold and saw footprints and dog paw prints in blood. Ms. Fisher stated Meredith told her Michelle was on her stomach and blood was spattered everywhere.[xi]

Now let's examine the **post**-911 phone calls. (911 call occurred at 1:25 p.m. and lasted approximately ten minutes)

- Linda called Meredith's cell phone at **1:36** (11 seconds).
- Meredith called Linda from the Young's house phone at **1:39**. The call lasted 1 minute, 43 seconds. The length of the call is inconsistent with "I'm at the salon. I'll call you back." Also, since it's an emergency, wouldn't Meredith have said "No, mom! It's an emergency!"? Also, just three minutes prior Linda was phoning Meredith. Was she really tied up with her hair appointment just three minutes later?
- Meredith called Colleen at **1:44** (25 seconds). She allegedly told Colleen to get to Michelle's ASAP. She did not inform her about Michelle.
- Meredith called Linda a second time at **1:47** (2 minute, 35 seconds). This is when, according to Meredith, Linda would have learned of Michelle's death. According to the police interview above, the conversation should have lasted longer. Linda would have been driving home from her hair appointment.
- Linda called Jason from her home phone at **1:53** and left him a message (44 seconds). Would she have arrived home and placed that call so quickly—just three minutes after hanging up with Meredith? It seems unlikely.

It seems more plausible that Linda learned the news during the pre-911 call at 1:07 and these calls are so important in understanding the timeline and sequence of events. Police questioned Linda again about the calls four months later. There must be a reason they were still examining the phone calls.

> I asked Linda to think back on November 3rd when she was notified about Michelle being found dead, if she remembered how she was notified, who notified her. She said Meredith called. She said she was using Jason Young's house phone. I asked Linda which phone did she call you on. She said it was on my cell phone. Linda said she was driving home. She remembers that she talked about it with her while driving.[xii]

Were they asking questions because the statements were inconsistent with the phone records? Linda's cell phone records are suspiciously absent from the discovery; however, her November 2005 records *are* present. The print is very small and it's possible the defense didn't notice that the wrong year's records were turned over. The records are important because they would verify the time that Linda made her flight reservation.

Police believed that Jason purposely created the print-out scenario as an excuse to send Meredith to the house to care for Cassidy. The problem with this theory is that he didn't call Meredith until after noon. Why would he have waited so long when he could have easily called her first thing in the morning? Considering how close he was to Cassidy, it is highly unlikely he would have left her loose in the house and then not even bothered to ensure that she was cared for until after noon. Further, would Jason have planned an overnight stay at his mother's home . . . risking the possibility that Meredith wouldn't be available to swing by the house that day? Wouldn't it have been more logical for him to head directly home following his meetings? Did he really need Meredith to discover the body if he'd killed Michelle? His alibi would have already been established.

It is possible that a different set of investigators would have analyzed the phone calls and not been so quick to overlook the possibility of Meredith's involvement, but then maybe there's a reason Linda's phone records are missing. Maybe they were withholding exculpatory evidence.

CHAPTER 12

Surveillance camera shenanigans

Shortly after Michelle's death, police interviewed the Hampton Inn staff where Jason had spent the night of November 2. They wanted to know everything. Were there food delivery options available? Did the USA Today newspapers arrive at the hotel with a Hampton Inn sticker, or did the staff affix it? Could Jason have received his receipt at arrival time? They were trying to determine if there was *any* possible way that he could have checked into the hotel to create an alibi and still obtain a receipt and newspaper sticker without actually spending the night there. They were coming up empty because the staff assured them that the newspapers arrived with the sticker already affixed and there was no possible way that Jason could have obtained his receipt at check-in. Receipts are placed under the guests' doors at approximately four o'clock each morning.

Detective Simmons with the Wake County Sheriff's Office interviewed manager, Jennifer Marshall in the winter of 2007. She informed Simmons that Keith Hicks worked the third shift that night and would have arrived for work at eleven o'clock. She was asked if anything out of the ordinary happened during Young's stay and she described that their maintenance worker Elmer Goad noticed one of the stairwell cameras had been unplugged.

Goad shared his account of the camera issue with the detective. He arrived at work shortly before six that morning and he and Hicks were in the back office when they noticed one of the cameras was dark. The monitor had one screen displaying four camera views. It alternated every second to display separate camera views throughout the property. Since there are twelve cameras, they don't see a constant feed from each individual camera. Goad said that once they identified that the stairwell camera was out, they both went to investigate it and found that it had been unplugged. Investigators would later determine that the camera went black at 11:20 p.m., which was approximately twenty-five minutes after Jason had checked in. Police wondered if Jason unplugged the camera to avoid being seen leaving the hotel.

Goad further described that he could not reach the camera to plug it back in and needed to use a ladder. He said he checked the camera monitor when he returned to the office and everything looked good. However, thirty or so minutes later, he noticed the camera was angled oddly because he could no longer see the stairs and exit door. He said that he and Hicks went back to the camera and noticed it was tilted toward the ceiling.

The possible camera tampering could look incriminating for Jason. The employees stated that it rarely happened. It *is* quite a coincidence that these issues occurred the very night of the murder when he happened to be there . . . but the clerk and maintenance workers' stories are inconsistent with the actual camera footage. In fact, the footage shows that Hicks is likely the person who tampered with the camera.

Investigators viewed the camera footage for the night in question and noted the time the camera went black and the time the image reappeared.

Also note that police observed that the camera displayed a tilted image at 5:50:14. That is inconsistent with Goad's story about returning to the desk and finding that the camera was tilted thirty minutes or so later. It was already tilted at the time it was plugged back in.

The investigator's observations also indicate that the camera was adjusted at 6:35. It makes sense that Goad noticed the camera was angled and then went to adjust it at that time. There is no indication that Goad ever went to plug the camera in. It's more logical that Hicks plugged it in since his face appeared on the feed right after the camera image returned and that he likely bumped it at that time as the notes indicate "camera is now tilted"

Analysis of the camera in question (source – Detective Brent David's summary):

11/02/06 23:20:13   Camera goes black.

11/03/06 **05:50:14**   **Camera image returns**, shows legs of person standing on landing, *camera is now tilted*.

11/03/06 05:55:43   **Face and body of Keith Hicks appears**.

11/03/06 06:16:41   Elmer Goad - maintenance person, appears to be walking down the stairs.

11/03/06 06:35:06   Camera moved and pointed toward emergency light.

11/03/06 06:37:06   Camera pointed toward the exit.

11/03/06 06:37:56   Camera has someone in front of it, appears to be repositioning it.

11/03/06 **06:38:10**   Camera pointed toward the stairs

    Maybe Hicks unplugged the camera shortly after arriving at work so he could sneak out that exit door at night to smoke cigarettes. An ash-tray is located outside that exit door. Then he plugged it back in shortly before the end of his shift.

    Detective Stubbs recorded observations about the *front* desk camera and noted that at 6:38 the clerk was behind the counter. This further disputes Goad's story—that he and Hicks went to investigate the camera together, because the camera was angled back toward the stairs at a time when Hicks was behind the desk. Goad must have adjusted it himself.

    It seems likely that police found a convenient way to attribute the camera shenanigans to Jason, but the detectives' notes dispute Elmer Goad's and Keith Hicks's stories.

    It is also interesting that Detective David's notes state that Goad "appears to be walking down the stairs" at

6:16, but then what did he do at that time? Nothing happens with the camera again until twenty minutes later, at which time the camera is supposedly angled differently. Was it *really* angled differently after it was plugged in? David's notes indicate "camera was tilted" at 5:50 when the camera image returned. It's likely it wasn't even Goad on the camera at 6:16. He certainly didn't fix a camera at that time. Note that the camera details were discovered by this author while researching the case files.

Just weeks after the murder, both Hicks and Goad were taken to a local police station and fingerprinted to determine whether either of them had touched the camera. At that point Hicks agreed to be printed because he stated that he did at one point plug in the camera. The suspicious camera story seemed to have evolved after that. Hicks' new story was that he discovered the unplugged camera during his shift and also noticed a rock propping open the exit door in the same area and that as soon as Goad arrived, he told him about the unplugged camera. The story doesn't work. It's clear that Hicks' had to admit that he was the one who plugged in (and likely unplugged) the camera when he submitted his prints.

For Jason to have pulled this off, he would have been dependent on both his room door and the emergency door remaining propped open all night while he went back to Raleigh. If anyone closed either of the doors, he's busted because then he's going to need a new key card to enter his room. He only used his key the one time shortly after check-in, so investigators needed a story that enabled him to leave and arrive back unnoticed. The flimsy "camera tampering/door propped open with a rock story" was it.

CHAPTER 12

2008

Investigators believed they made a break-through in the case in the early part of 2008. As previously mentioned, two different types of bloody shoe prints were found on some pillows near Michelle's body. One of them was easily identified from an outsole database as a Franklin athletic shoe sold by Family Dollar stores. It was also determined to be a size ten and the shoes were only sold in men's styles.

The other shoe print proved much more difficult to identify. There was only a partial section visible and it left a distinct heart-shaped impression. Thus far, no matches were identified in database searches. It was sent to the F.B.I. in the latter part of 2007, and in January 2008 F.B.I Agent Michael Smith reported that he'd identified the type of shoe that had left the second impression on the pillow—Hushpuppy Sealy. The shoe had been discontinued, but investigators were able to obtain one from the manufacturer for comparison purposes. An element from the sole appeared to match the one at the crime scene.

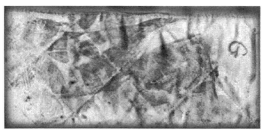
Second shoe print from crime scene

Hushpuppy Sealy impression

Investigators checked all of the available shoes that had been left in the cargo area of Jason's Explorer and also examined surveillance images from November 2 to see if they could identify the type of shoes he was wearing. They weren't able to find any shoes that matched.

Police then reviewed all of the Youngs' shoe purchases based on credit card records and determined that Jason had purchased a pair of size twelve Hushpuppy Orbital shoes from a DSW store in 2005. The Orbital model was manufactured specifically for DSW, but the outsole pattern was determined to be the same as the Sealy model. This meant that the pair of shoes purchased by Jason a year and a half before the murder could have left that shoe print found at the crime scene.

Since there were no discernible shoe impressions on the master bedroom carpet, it was impossible to accurately determine the size of the shoe, but it was estimated to be a size eleven or twelve. While they couldn't *match* the shoe to Jason, investigators believed this was significant circumstantial evidence that the bloody shoe impressions were left by him.

***

In February 2008, shortly after the identification of the second shoe print, police obtained a search warrant for the homes of Jason's sister and mother. They were looking for all of the shoes purchased by the Youngs in 2005, Michelle's wedding rings, missing items from her jewelry box and any cash gas receipts. There was one more item listed on the search warrant—a dark colored pullover garment with a lighter colored thin stripe bisecting the chest area. Jason was seen wearing the pullover on the surveillance video at the Hampton Inn.

Police had the surveillance video since November 2006, so why were they just now conducting a search for the shirt? Detective David's hand written notes contained a notation about the clothing.

> Review videotapes from Cracker Barrel in Greensboro, North Carolina and Hampton Inn in Hillsville, Virginia to see what clothes he is wearing and locate the same clothes in luggage seized during search warrant of Jason Young's Explorer. **Completed on 2/07/07**

If they had been unable to locate the shirt, why did the detective not mention that in February '07? Why didn't they obtain a search warrant at *that* time? Was the shirt really missing, or did police fail to properly inventory the item when they searched the Explorer? There were other items obtained from the vehicle that were never entered on an evidence sheet, such as the maps Jason had printed in preparation for his trip.

Nonetheless, neither the Hushpuppy shoes nor the dark pull-over were located in the search. Police collected several pairs of shoes, but didn't find any that matched the prints found at the crime scene.

***

The public rarely sees things from the perspective of one accused of a crime. Remember that Jason Young is presumed innocent at this point. His attorney, Roger Smith continued to advise him to remain silent, but that did not mean he was guilty. Right or wrong, he trusted the advice of his attorney, but doing so meant he had no ability to influence public perception. People believe a person is hiding something if they don't cooperate with police. All of the search warrants are public records and the media reports exactly what police are looking at. This was a high profile case, so when police searched his family's homes, the public knew about it.

Few realize what Jason and his family endured throughout the investigation. Assuming he's innocent, he was going about a normal day like any other and his whole world fell apart when he learned the shocking news of Michelle's death. He lost his young wife, his unborn son and the life he'd lived in Raleigh. The Fishers instantly accused him of murder. He had to move away from his friends, he couldn't talk to anyone about the case and it became isolating. To make matters worse, an internet vigilante group led by a man named Alan Banner became so convinced that Jason was guilty that they made things very difficult for Jason. Banner not only posted about his belief of Jason's guilt, he harassed him and his family and friends. Members of the witch-hunt internet group contacted Jason's employers, making it difficult for him to maintain employment. No one wanted to be associated with a murder suspect.

Banner viewed the autopsy photos. He went to Brevard and took pictures of Jason's family's homes. He posted yearbook pictures of Jason and his family. He sent harassing emails to friends and family. Some had to file restraining orders. Police had to tell Banner to leave them alone.

Jason's inability to maintain employment meant that his family had to support him and Cassidy financially.

He lived with Heather and Joe for a year and throughout most of that time they provided food, clothing and shelter. When they moved in with Pat, she provided for them. He had to continue making mortgage payments on the Birchleaf home and he'd lost the renters at the townhouse he still owned, so he also had to come up with money to cover that. His family bore a great financial burden as a result.

***

A "Ladybug Liftoff" <u>event</u> was organized in May, 2008 to honor Michelle's memory. This was likely an attempt to keep the case in the public eye.

Meredith had lost a considerable amount of weight by that point and seemed to have achieved her goal of fitting into Michelle's clothes.

Left to right: Detective Spivey, Linda Fisher, Meredith Fisher

Left to right: Meredith Fisher, Detective Spivey, Sheriff Donnie Harrison, Detective Blackwell, Linda Fisher

The tension between the Youngs and Fishers escalated that year. After Linda's emotional outburst during the visit with Cassidy in the spring of 2007, Jason felt it best to shield Cassidy from her and Meredith. As a result, they wouldn't see her for an entire year, and then, without Jason's permission, Linda and Meredith showed up at Cassidy's daycare center on her fourth birthday. They took cupcakes and balloons and were permitted to see her. When Jason learned of this, he told the director that they did not have permission to visit his daughter, but that didn't stop them. They went back again on a day when the director was absent and lied. They said they had permission to see her and again were allowed in. It was a "spa day" for Mother's Day and Cassidy got to apply make-up to Meredith and Linda. After that, Linda and Meredith hired family law attorney, Mike Schilawski. He sent Jason a letter in August

2008 informing him that he was hired to negotiate a visitation schedule on their behalf.

On October 29, 2008 a separate law firm—Michaels and Michaels filed a wrongful death suit against Jason on Linda's behalf. The claims were as follows:

- In the early morning hours of November 3, 2006, Jason Young brutally murdered Michelle Young at their residence.
- Plaintiff brings this action under N.C. Gen. Stat 28A-18-2 for the wrongful death of Michelle Young.
- Pursuant to 31A-3 and declaratory judgment rights under Article 26 of Chapter 1 of the General Statutes of North Carolina, plaintiff also seeks a determination by this court that Jason Young willfully and unlawfully killed Michelle Young or was an accessory before the fact in her murder.
- Whether Jason Young is determined to be Michelle Young's slayer through this action or through the criminal process, as also provided in 31A-3, plaintiff seeks a judgment declaring that Jason Young is barred from collecting any insurance benefits, that Jason Young is subject to all the provisions of Article 3 of Chapter 31A, and directing distribution of any applicable assets or benefits in accordance with said law.

- At the time of her death, Michelle Young was 29 years of age, pregnant and in excellent health.
- Michelle Young was the loving and devoted mother of Cassidy Young, who is the beneficiary of this wrongful death claim.
- Michelle Young was a Certified Public Accountant and an employee of Progress Energy.
- As a direct and proximate result of Defendant's murder of Michelle Young or his complicity in the murder, plaintiff is entitled to recover of Defendant all damages available under G.S. 28A-18-2, including but not limited to:
    - Compensation for the horror, pain and suffering of Michelle Young caused by defendant's fatal assault
    - The reasonable funeral expenses for Michelle Young
    - The present monetary value to Cassidy of her mother's reasonably expected net income
    - The present monetary value to Cassidy for the loss of her mother's reasonably expected services, protection care and assistance.
    - The present monetary value to Cassidy of her mother's reasonably expected society, companionship,

- comfort, guidance, kindly offices and advice, and
  - Punitive damages for the murder of Michelle Young.
- Plaintiff, in her capacity as Executrix for the estate of Michelle Marie Fisher Young, is entitled to recover from defendant compensatory damages in an amount in excess of ten thousand dollars.
- Plaintiff, in her capacity as Executrix for the estate of Michelle Marie Fisher Young is entitled to recover from defendant punitive damages in an amount in excess of ten thousand dollars.

Wherefore, plaintiff, Linda Fisher, in her capacity as Executrix for the estate of Michelle Marie Fisher Young, respectfully prays to the court for judgment as follows:

- That this Court find, pursuant to 31A-3 of the General Statutes of North Carolina, that Jason Young willfully and unlawfully killed Michelle Young or was an accessory before the fact of her murder.
- Whether Jason Young is determined Michelle Young's slayer through this action or the criminal process, a judgment declaring that Jason Young was the slayer of Michelle Young.

- A judgment declaring that Jason Young is barred from collecting any life insurance benefits on the life of Michelle Young.
- A judgment declaring, directing and applying all applicable provisions of article 3 of Chapter 31A of the North Carolina General Statutes.
- That plaintiff have and recover from defendant, Jason Young, compensatory damages for the wrongful death of Michelle Marie Fisher Young in an amount in excess of ten thousand dollars.
- That plaintiff have and recover from the defendant the costs of court, including interest, to the extent permitted by law
- That plaintiff have such and further relief which the Court deems equitable, just and proper.

It is highly unusual to see a wrongful death suit precede the criminal process, but what it does is lock the accused into a lose/lose scenario. Civil suits are great for the prosecutors who are hoping to indict a person for a crime. If the accused responds to the suit, they must submit to a lengthy deposition where they are forced to give up their silence and respond to *all* questions. In another local case, Brad Cooper responded to a custody suit while he was being investigated for the murder of his wife and he had to endure seven straight hours of questioning. He was asked about every specific detail about his life—from what type of allergy medications he took to intimate details about his sexual relations. The deposition was then scrutinized by police as they searched for any inconsistency or red flag to justify an arrest. The deposition was also public record so it was aired on the website of a local news station. Cooper's private life was completely exposed and it was used to taint his reputation and help the state win a conviction.

If Jason responded to the wrongful death suit, it would probably cost him hundreds of thousands of dollars in legal fees, money that he did not have. Since it is a civil proceeding, court appointed counsel is not an option.

Assuming he did have the money, what were his odds of winning a wrongful death suit? Well, lead detective Richard Spivey filed an affidavit on behalf of plaintiff, Linda Fisher stating the following:

> I have been provided a copy of the Complaint in this civil case. Based on my experience in law enforcement, which is set forth in detail in Exhibit A and B, and my knowledge of the evidence gathered in the investigation of the death of Michelle Young, <u>in my opinion the allegation in the Complaint that "in the early morning hours of November 3, 2006, Jason Young brutally murdered Michelle Young at their residence" is true.</u>[xiii]

The detective filed the affidavit with no evidence to support the claim. There was nothing tying Jason Young to the murder. They didn't have enough evidence to charge him, just a bunch of unsubstantiated circumstantial evidence and the fact that he'd had an affair, but that didn't matter with regard to the civil case. Everything was stacked against him because not only did police state that they believed the allegation was true, the district attorney's office supplied Linda's attorney, Paul Michaels with all of the police discovery. All of the search warrants and investigative documents were attached to the claim. The government was thus assisting the victim's family in the civil lawsuit, making it impossible for Jason to win. No judge would rule in favor of a defendant under those circumstances. Jason had absolutely no choice but to ignore the claim.

The timing was calculated as well. The statute of limitations on a wrongful death suit is two years. They filed just days before the anniversary of Michelle's death. That meant that the Youngs couldn't file their own wrongful death suit against Meredith. It was too late.

A defendant has thirty days to respond to a wrongful death suit. At such time, the plaintiff can ask the court to issue a default judgment. The judge does not have to enter a judgment at this time. They can delay pending the outcome of the criminal case, but that's not what happened. On December 5, 2008 Judge Donald Stephens declared Jason Young a "slayer" barring him from any life insurance proceeds and deeming him subject to punitive and compensatory damages.

> It is therefore ordered, adjudged and decreed <u>that the defendant, Jason Lynn Young willfully and unlawfully killed Plaintiff's decdent, Michelle Marie Fisher Young, within the definition of "slayer"</u>

under General Statute 31A-3(3)d; that under General Statute 31-A-11 the defendant, Jason Lynn Young is barred from collecting the proceeds of any inssurance on the life of Michelle Marie Fisher Young and that any insurance payable to defendant Jason Lynn Young, by virtue of his surviving Michelle Marie Fisher Young shall be paid to the person or persons who would have been entitled thereto if Jason Lynn Young had predeceased Michelle Marie Fisher Young or to the Estate of Michelle Marie Fisher Young if not alternate beneficiary is named, and that the defendant, Jason Lynn Young, is barred from testate or intestate succession from the Estate of Michelle Marie Fisher Young under G.S. 31A-4 and is deemed to have died immediately prior to Michelle Fisher Young.

It is further ordered adjuged and decreed that there is no just reason for delaying the entry of this judgement as a final judgement and under Rule 54(b) this judgment is hereby entered as a final judgement.
The Court acknowledges that Plaintiff's remaining claims against the defendant beyond those adjudicated herein remain pending.[xiv]

  Jason and Michelle held a two million dollar life insurance policy on each other. It was Michelle's idea to get the insurance policies and she had her sorority sister who was an attorney write up the policies. Since Jason had lost his father at such a young age, he wanted to ensure that his daughter and future children would never have to worry about money. Due to the circumstances of Michelle's death, the plan had a double indemnity clause so the insurance value was four million dollars. Cassidy would inherit the money at age twenty-one, but first the lawyer received $1,063,000 and Linda received $156,000 as Executrix of Michelle's Estate. Consider the ramifications of this if Jason Young is innocent.

CHAPTER 14

2009

Things got much worse for Jason when Linda and Meredith filed for primary custody of Cassidy just two weeks after the wrongful death judgment was signed. I suppose Linda's comment at the funeral, "I'm going to get you!" was coming to fruition. Again, if Jason responded, he would be forced to submit to a deposition—depriving him of his Fifth Ammendment right to remain silent. Again, there was no way he could win the custody suit because Linda had police and prosecutors on her side, filing affidavits and willing to hand over all the discovery files to her attorney.

It was agreed that in September 2009, Cassidy would live with Meredith and begin Kindergarten in Wake County. Meredith would also receive the sum of $3700 per month from Cassidy's estate to pay for her expenses. There was nothing Jason could do to prevent this. If he'd had any idea these suits were coming, he could have arranged for his sister, Heather to adopt Cassidy but it was too late for that. In March 2009 a judge ordered Jason Young to pay

Linda Fisher $15.6 million in the wrongful death of Michelle Young.

The abuse of legal procedures in this case can not be overstated. It was unconstitutional to threaten Jason Young in this manner. He was being forced to give up his Fifth Ammendment right to remain silent in order to maintain custody of his daughter. What differentiates this case from many is the fact that police and the District Attorney aligned with the plaintiff (Linda Fisher) to influence the proceeding. Detective Spivey signed an affidavit and testifed that it was his *opinion* that Jason Young murdered his wife. The District Attorney handed all of the investigative case files to Linda's attorney. Though the attorneys handled the proceedings, with the State behind them, it amounted to a criminal process but the defendant had no right to a public defender and therefore no way to answer to the complaints. It was a gross abuse of power and shouldn't be allowed.

Shortly after the wrongful death judgement was handed down, Linda and Meredith showed up at Jason's storage facility. His possessions from the Birchleaf home were stored at the facility since he was staying with family. The Fishers supposedly had a document that entitled them to any and all of Jason's assets as a result of the civil suit judgment. Whether it was legitimate or not, they were given access to the shed. Jason and his family were unsure exactly what all was taken, but would later learn that Meredith had taken the jewelry box with the two missing drawers—the item related to the crime. It is shocking that investigators hadn't collected it into evidence during the early investigation, but why would Meredith want it? The box was a gift from Pat Young to Michelle. Pat had it made especially for Michelle, so it shouldn't have held any special meaning to Meredith. It's very suspicious. Did she have the other two drawers? Was she worried it may have contained evidence that could incriminate her? Investigators collected the jewelry box from Meredith in the fall of 2011.

Over the next several months, Meredith and Linda had regular visits with Cassidy and in September, she went to live with Meredith full time in Fuquay-Varina. Jason had Cassidy on weekends and holidays.

Jason was arrested on December 16, 2009 and charged with first degree murder. He was appointed a public defender as he could no longer afford his attorney. His arrest didn't follow any new compelling evidence. They had nothing more than they'd had in January, 2008 when they discovered the type of shoe print left near the body. What prompted the arrest? Was the prosecution relying on the prejudice from the back to back civil suits to win a conviction? Could Jason Young receive a fair trial?

CHAPTER 15

Trial

Note: Having viewed the entire trial and researched the case files, the author will occasionally include first person narratives to describe pertinent details that were not revealed in court.

The trial began on June 7, 2011 at the Wake county courthouse in Raleigh. It was just short of a month since Brad Cooper was convicted of murdering his wife—another high profile case in which police aligned with the plaintiff in a custody lawsuit before criminal charges were filed. In an equally weak case with little evidence, Cooper didn't fare well against the power of officials who were willing to do anything to win. The community followed the case closely and the trial was streamed online by local news station, WRAL.

Assistant district attorney (ADA) Rebecca (Becky) Holt delivered opening arguments for the state. Holt described the Young's marriage as volatile, especially due to the mounting tension from Linda Fisher's increasing presence in the couple's lives — *motive*. She talked about Alan Fisher's last minute cancellation in plans to visit Jason and Michelle — *opportunity*. She referenced the camera shenanigans from the Hampton Inn — *means*. There was little discussion about the evidence against Young. Did they have enough to convince a jury of his guilt?

Defense attorney Mike Klinkosum's opening arguments were much more compelling, with concise details about the evidence. He first highlighted the *absence* of evidence. Michelle fought hard enough against her attackers that she sustained defensive wounds on her hands and wrists, yet Jason didn't have a single scratch or bruise on his entire body. No blood was found in his vehicle or hotel room, despite an extremely bloody crime scene. Investigators even searched for fiber transfers between the home and his hotel room—nothing.

This would be an interesting trial and Websleuths was buzzing with activity as the "Jason is guilty" people argued with those who either believed Jason was innocent or were withholding judgment pending testimony.

Though the burden of proof lies with the state, it is not so simple anymore. Prosecutors are known to trick jurors by presenting a string of circumstances that, on their own are completely innocuous, yet they often manage to convince jurors that the long list of "coincidences" are red flags. Few realize that circumstantial evidence must be *fact based* to count as evidence of guilt, and this is one of the biggest factors in wrongful convictions. Jurors don't even realize they are being manipulated. Pay close attention to each piece of evidence offered by the state and consider whether or not it qualifies as circumstantial evidence—is it fact based or not?

The state called their star witness, Meredith Fisher to testify first. She described Jason's and Michelle's fighting, her recent role as mediator and how she came to find her sister's body. The prosecution wanted the jury to believe that it was unusual for Jason to have sent Meredith to the house that day. They also wanted them to know that Jason didn't talk to police when he arrived back in town that evening. The cross-examination was much more interesting as all of Meredith's inconsistencies were pointed out:

- She stated that the dog was inside the house, yet no paw prints were found.
- She testified that she went home after leaving the Ale House, yet there is surveillance video of her at Sheetz.
- She testified that she arrived home at 3, but she was actually at Sheetz until 3:59.
- She told police she called Colleen from Sheetz at 2:27, but she didn't actually arrive there until 3:37.
- She initially said her key didn't work in the front door, then later told police she didn't actually have the key with her that day.
- She initially told police she arrived at the house at 1:00, but the 911 call wasn't placed until 1:25.
- She testified on direct that her keys were on the kitchen counter. They didn't question her about the keys on the hood of Michelle's Lexus, even though she'd identified the keys as hers.

- She initially told police that she'd called Jason about an hour after finding Michelle. She had not called him that afternoon and didn't speak to him until he called Colleen's phone to try to reach her that evening.
- She didn't give police Cassidy's t-shirt. Why would she have left that shirt on her? She later gave police *a* pink t-shirt and said she had washed it. It's impossible to know if it was the same one Michelle had put on her that night.
- They pointed out the multiple police interviews to question her about inconsistencies, phone calls, the 911 call and her failure to roll Michelle over.

The inconsistencies are significant because the state asserts that only Jason would have cleaned up Cassidy, a stranger surely wouldn't do that . . . but Meredith would. She was in a position to do so, plus her alibi that night was never verified. However, while the defense pointed out the red flags, they never came out and stated that she should have been investigated as a suspect. Instead they hoped the jurors would consider the possibility after hearing the inconsistencies in her story.

The prosecution spent an entire day questioning the Hampton Inn employees. They called the clerk who checked Jason in, the night clerk, the manager and the maintenance worker. It was ridiculous. Did they really need to provide testimony that Jason Young checked into the hotel that night? It wasn't disputed. The receipt was in his vehicle, charge was on his credit statement. Even the defense failed to point out that the camera story simply didn't work. It was inconsistent with the facts.

The prosecution elicited testimony from the clerk and maintenance worker that suggested that something very odd happened that night—the exit door camera was mysteriously unplugged and a rock was found propping open the stairwell door. Remember from Chapter 12 that the story doesn't work based on the investigator's observations while viewing the footage that night. However, the notes were not revealed at trial so the story was not disputed by the defense.

Goad testified that shortly after arriving at work that morning, he and Hicks noticed the camera wasn't working and together they went to investigate it. Hicks' testimony was inconsistent with Goad's. He testified that he noticed the camera was unplugged when he was delivering the newspapers to the guests' doors that morning and then he waited for Goad to arrive to inform him about the unplugged camera. Why then did Goad testify that the two of them identified the camera issue *together* after he'd arrived to work that morning? The testimony can't be trusted, but again it wasn't disputed.

The defense pointed out that Jason was seen on the front desk camera just before midnight and walking down the corridor toward the exit door shortly after the camera would have been unplugged. Is there any logical reason why he would have unplugged the exit door camera at 11:23 p.m., and then later went back to areas where he would be clearly seen on camera? How was that concealing his ability to "sneak" out of the hotel that night? It was not logical.

The defense also pointed out that Jason wouldn't have had any knowledge of how the cameras operated. As it turns out the Hampton Inn cameras cycle so that an image is captured at each camera and then it moves to the next, and so on. There are approximately a dozen cameras on the property. So IF Jason had unplugged the camera as part of a scheme to leave unnoticed, how would he have known that he wouldn't be captured by that camera *while unplugging it*?! It doesn't make sense that anyone would be stupid enough to do this to avoid being seen.

The camera was swabbed for DNA and dusted for prints. A DNA profile was obtained, but it did not match Jason Young, nor were his fingerprints found on the camera. The state could not prove that Jason tampered with the camera; therefore it is not circumstantial evidence tying him to the murder. Had they identified his fingerprints on the camera, then it would have qualified as circumstantial evidence.

The prosecution was counting on a jury willing to convict based on "could haves." They asserted that Jason *could have* tampered with the camera, though no proof was ever provided. They used the camera testimony to show that Jason Young had opportunity to commit the murder, but a careful examination by the author revealed that the Hampton Inn employees' stories don't work. The camera tampering images with times were not included in court exhibits. Had they been, the jury would have likely arrived at the same conclusion. Also remember that for Jason to have pulled this off, he would have been dependent on both the exit door *and* his hotel room door remaining propped open all night long, because naturally he couldn't very well swipe his key to enter the property at six or seven o'clock that morning. That would be evidence that he could have left the hotel. This murder plan defies all logic and common sense.

Next, *4 Brothers* clerk, Gracie Bailey testified that she identified Jason Young as the man who threw down a twenty dollar bill and cussed at her at approximately 5:20 the morning of November 3. This is the only witness who places Jason away from the hotel that night. The defense refuted her testimony with ease as they pointed out that she had been interviewed on four separate occasions and not once gave a description of the person she'd allegedly identified from the photo shown by the detectives when they were canvassing stores just days after Michelle's death. More significantly, during a pre-trial hearing Gracie was asked to describe the obnoxious customer believed to be Jason Young. She described him as someone who had a "little bit of hair" and "a little taller than me." Gracie was five feet tall. Jason Young was over six feet tall with a full head of hair. Nonetheless, clearly the prosecutions' case was so weak that they were dependent on this witness to try to convince the jury that Jason Young was at a location that was consistent with their timeline.

***

Physical Evidence: DNA, Fingerprints, Hair, Fibers, and Shoe Prints

SBI Agent, Karen Morrow testified about the two shoe prints found in blood on the pillows. Recall that the print had been identified as a size 10 athletic shoe sold at Dollar General stores. Morrow was tasked with identifying the second print. She testified about how FBI Agent Michael Smith finally identified the print through the FBI's database, over a year after the murder. The Hushpuppy Sealy appeared to have the same heart shaped element on the sole as the print on the pillow.

Agent Smith consulted with Tom Riha, director of product development at Wolverine Worldwide—Hushpuppy's parent company. Riha agreed that the print could have been made by a Hushpuppy Sealy or Bellville shoe which had the same sole and that the Orbital shoe purchased by Jason in 2005 had the identical outsole.

A size eight Hushpuppy Sealy shoe was sent to Agent Morrow from the manufacturer and prints were cast to compare to those left on the pillow. It was *possible* that that type of shoe made the impression, but due to the limited detail, a more conclusive comparison could not be made. Was this strong enough to convince a jury?

After reviewing the case materials and trial testimony, the author wishes there had been more confirmation that the Orbital sole was identical to that of the Sealy and Belleville. Surely DSW would have had photos of the Orbital sole. It doesn't appear that anyone obtained any documentation confirming this. They simply took the word of the witness. What if he was mistaken? Also, Wolverine owned several shoe companies and manufactured millions of shoes per year. How common was this particular outsole design? Was it used in their other shoe lines? No one asked these questions.

Of significance is the fact that when police seized Jason's Explorer, they found a pair of Kenneth Cole slip-on casual shoes in the cargo area. The style of shoe was similar to the Hushpuppy Orbitals purchased in 2005. It seems logical therefore that Jason purchased the Kenneth Cole shoes to replace the worn-out Orbitals. If he was wearing the Orbital shoes the night of the murder, why did he have another pair of the same style shoes in his vehicle? It would have been interesting to see when the Kenneth Cole shoes were purchased, but there was no evidence that investigators ever sought that information.

Jason Young's shoes from Explorer

It's likely that Jason was wearing the Kenneth Cole shoes during his trip to Virginia. When he arrived in Raleigh he was wearing dressier shoes since he had visited customers that afternoon.

If the casual shoes he was seen wearing at the Cracker Barrel were missing, then investigators could speculate that they *could have* been the missing Orbitals, but that wasn't the case. Also, there is no explanation offered by the State to explain the *two* sets of prints. Two types of prints indicate that two people committed the crime. The shoe evidence probably qualifies as weak circumstantial evidence, because the print *could have* been left by a pair of shoes once owned by Jason Young. It's weak because there's not a characteristic of the print that definitively ties to the specific pair of Orbital shoes once purchased by Jason Young and there is evidence that he clearly purchased a new pair of casual slip-on shoes some time after the Orbital purchase in the summer of 2005.

The prosecution made a big deal about the fact that Jason purchased a pair of casual slip-on shoes just days after the murder, but obviously he needed things since he didn't have anything but the clothes on his back.

***

Though C.C.B.I. collected several items for DNA analyses, there was only a brief amount of evidence presented at trial. Since the crime occurred in Jason Young's home, it was natural to find his DNA at the scene. DNA results were presented from the following items: the rock which was allegedly used to prop open the Hampton Inn exit door, a slab of sheetrock from the area near Michelle's body, a section of the closet's molding, swabs from the sprinkler at the Hampton Inn, and swabs from the jewelry box with the missing two drawers.

LabCorp analyst Shawn Weiss was able to extract three of nine DNA markers from the rock and stated that he could not exclude Jason as the contributor, but it was very weak evidence because many people in the population would share those three markers. Jason could not be excluded as the contributor of the DNA found on the sheetrock from the crime scene and the section of closet molding from Jason's closet, but this was no surprise since he lived in the house. Jason was excluded as the contributor to the DNA found on the sprinkler at the Hampton Inn. This is important because the sprinkler was near the camera that had been tampered with. The DNA from the jewelry box was the most interesting. A mixed profile was found that did not match Jason or Michelle. One of the contributors was female. It would be very interesting to see that particular profile matched up against all of the standards collected in this case. The profile was only compared against Jason's and Michelle's profiles.

The North Carolina crime lab obtained a partial profile of Cassidy's DNA on a medicine dropper found on the hutch in her bedroom. A small amount of red liquid remained in the dropper. A bottle of red liquid Tylenol was next to the dropper. Police had a theory that Cassidy may have been given medication so she would sleep, but an unidentified fingerprint was found on the Tylenol medicine cap. Police were very thorough in collecting prints from everyone who had ever been in the Young's house. They collected over a hundred standards. None of them matched the print on the medicine cap.

None of the hairs found at the crime scene matched Jason's. A clump of approximately fifty hairs were found under Michelle's body, demonstrating the severity of the struggle. Some had been forcibly removed and still retained the root. They were all determined to be Michelle's. A single strand of hair found in Michelle's hand also belonged to her.

Remember that Dr. Godwin found several pieces of evidence that investigators had failed to collect. One item was a hair on a photo frame from the dresser adjacent to Michelle's body. The crime lab determined that it had been forcibly removed. The DNA did not match Michelle or Jason or any other profile generated in this case. Could it hold the key to solving this crime? Perhaps it could be re-run through CODIS to see if a match is generated. Several years have now passed since the investigation.

The state crime lab did a thorough fiber analysis. Tapings of several items were conducted to look for fiber transfers. Investigators searched the crime scene items for transfer fibers from the Hampton Inn to see if they could place Jason at the scene. That was unsuccessful despite a thorough examination. Tapings from the Hampton Inn carpeting, bed spread and sheets were collected. Tapings from Cassidy's and Michelle's clothing, the pillows, carpeting and bedding were all examined.

In addition to the unidentified prints on the Tylenol medicine cup, some were also found on a shoe-shine box in Jason's closet as well as the Hampton Inn camera. The prints on the shoe-shine box could have been left by the killer. The closet had clearly been rummaged through. Jason's wallet with five-hundred dollars cash was missing. The killer had to move Michelle's body to get inside the closet.

Regarding the camera tampering, the state wanted to hold Jason accountable for that, despite prints and DNA pointing to someone else. This was a key factor of their theory because it placed him outside the hotel that night. It demonstrates how prosecutors can build a case against someone, even when forensic evidence excludes them—absence of evidence.

Condoms were found in two locations of the house—one was on the living room table, the other was on the floor next to the dresser near the body. C.C.B.I specifically requested a sexual assault kit from the medical examiner, but it was not completed. It is unclear why this request was ignored. It's possible he opted against it since the victim was found fully dressed, but one would have expected this test since investigators requested it. Jason and Michelle did not use condoms, but one of Jason's thumb prints was found on one of the condoms. The other did not contain any discernible prints. It's odd that condoms would have been lying out like that. It's doubtful the Youngs kept them on the living room table.

***

Character Assassination

With so little evidence, the prosecution used character assassination to influence the jury. Does a bad husband equal a brutal murderer? All of the witnesses who knew Jason and Michelle were asked about their relationship and many stated that they argued a lot, though no one testified that Jason had ever harmed Michelle. The few times when fights became physical, it was Michelle who had physically attacked Jason. He'd gotten scratches to prove it. He was concerned enough about the attacks that he'd confided in Alan Fisher. Jason told Alan several months before her death that if it happened again, he would leave her.

Witnesses also testified about Jason's immature, obnoxious behaviors, especially when he would drink too much, but friends were willing to overlook these things because he was fun and likeable.

Jason's ex-fiancée, Genevieve "Genny" Cargol testified for the state. She and Jason began dating in 1997 while they both attended NC State and became engaged in 1999 with plans to marry in 2000. Genny recalled an incident that occurred sometime after they'd gotten engaged. They attended a wedding together in Texas. Many of Jason's friends had also traveled to Texas to attend the wedding so they thought it would be fun to get together the evening before the wedding. There were several couples there and everyone was having fun until Jason and a buddy decided to play some drinking games. He had several beers and a couple shots on top of that. Genny was not happy about it. She did not like it when Jason drank too much.

Soon they all headed back to the hotel. Genny described how Jason passed out for a good hour. When he woke up they got into a bad argument about his drinking. She reminded him that he'd promised not to drink too much. At that point, Jason told her that if she didn't believe he would make a good husband, they should just call off the wedding plans. He wanted the engagement ring back. Genny swore she couldn't remove it because it was too tight. She said at that point Jason threw her around the room and ultimately pinned her down and took the ring off her finger. She said she had bruises on her arms and rib cage from the fight. The testimony was damaging because there was an inference that Jason had a pattern of removing women's rings. Michelle's wedding rings had been taken.

Of course the alleged bruising also sounded bad, since Michelle had been beaten to death.

They ended up getting through the wedding and by the end of the weekend Genny really wanted her ring back. She begged Jason for the ring, but he told her he wanted to think about it for a while. Would she have begged for the ring back if things had been as brutal as she'd described? Jason finally gave it back to her the day after the wedding. They continued the relationship, but it was off and on for about a year and they ended up breaking up for good.

Next the prosecutors called Molly Crawford and Amanda Thompson back to back. Molly was of course asked to discuss her relationship with Jason—how they'd become close, the daily phone calls to each other and the intimate weekend they'd shared just a month before Michelle's death. It wasn't good for Jason either, but there was no plan in place for Jason and Molly to be together. They lived in different states and both were married with young children. Investigators never found any evidence that the affair was a motive for murder. Molly described how she'd spoken to Jason the evening of November 2, and he was completely normal. They spoke at just before midnight and he wasn't rushed to get off the phone or anything. It certainly didn't seem like he had plans to drive all the way back to Raleigh to kill his wife.

Following Michelle's death, Molly hadn't spoken to Jason for months, but they reconnected in June. They were both in Myrtle Beach for another group get-together and they talked for hours. Molly felt like Jason was the only person who could relate to what she had been through with the harassment from police and media and the isolation it had caused. They began talking by phone again regularly, but the nature of their relationship had changed. They were strictly friends. However, the friendship ended abruptly months later after the police visited Molly once again. This time they showed up with an SBI agent. The agent was rough on Molly. He called her an idiot for associating with Jason and was firm when he told her that if she didn't cut off contact with him, she would be going down as an accessory. She had no choice but to end all ties with Jason. Molly maintained her composure throughout her testimony, but it was clear that the investigation had taken a toll on her and her family.

Amanda's testimony was heartbreaking to watch. She was clearly humiliated, distraught and on the verge of tears throughout her testimony. The prosecution had her share the "swallowed wedding ring" story and then surprisingly got her to admit that she'd slept with Jason during her October visit to Raleigh. Oddly, this detail was not included in any of the police reports from interviews. Police had even flown out to Montana to meet with her in person and there was no mention of the sexual encounter. Nonetheless, this testimony was damaging, and this was yet another odd association to wedding rings. It was painful to watch this testimony and Amanda had to inform her husband that she'd slept with Jason before the trial. Did the prosecution accomplish anything? Did her testimony do anything to connect Jason to Michelle's death or did they use this because they didn't have any evidence?

***

The prosecution used a story about a car accident the Youngs had experienced during the spring of 2006 to suggest that Jason had intentionally caused the wreck. Jason, Michelle and Cassidy went to Brevard Memorial Day weekend. Michelle had just discovered she was pregnant the prior week. She was overjoyed and she shared the news with Jason by dressing Cassidy in a t-shirt that said "I'm going to be a big sister." She went to the doctor a few days later and an ultrasound was performed to date the pregnancy. A fetal sac was visible, but no sign of a fetal pole was found. It was possible that it was too early to see anything and the doctor told Michelle to return on June 5 for a second scan. She was to visit the doctor just after the trip to Brevard.

Jason and Michelle woke up Sunday morning and decided to head into town for some coffee. They left Cassidy with his mom. At one point, Jason over-corrected on a bend and their car went down an embankment and into a river. It was a very frightening experience for both of them, but they were able to get out of the car safely and call for help. They went to the hospital, but luckily neither had sustained injuries from the accident.

Upon returning home to Raleigh, Michelle saw her doctor for the second ultrasound, but it was clear that the baby hadn't developed as expected. According to her medical records, it was classified as a "missed" miscarriage. She was told to have a procedure known as a D&E (dilation and evacuation), which is the prescribed procedure in cases like this. Naturally Michelle was devastated, but she quickly became pregnant again the next month and everything went well with that pregnancy, however, the testimony was misleading as it suggested that the car wreck had caused the pregnancy loss. There was no testimony provided about how early Michelle's pregnancy was and the unlikelihood that the car accident had caused the miscarriage.

The story was derived from a police interview with Meredith just days after Michelle's death. She brought up the accident as she was casting suspicion on Jason from the very beginning.

> Meredith also wanted to inform me of a traffic accident that her sister and brother-in-law had been involved in the late spring, possibly May of 2006. Meredith explained Michelle and Jason were at Jason's mother's home in Brevard. They had gotten up that morning to go get coffee and had left Cassidy at Jason's mother's home. During their drive Michelle had unbuckled her seatbelt to reach down to get something off the floorboard of the car. At that moment Jason lost control of the vehicle and the vehicle drove off the cliff. The two were able to get out unharmed but Michelle who was pregnant at the time lost the child. (Meredith Fisher 11/14/06 interview with Detective David)

Clearly the prosecution believed it would work to their advantage to influence the jury, even though they must have been aware that the pregnancy loss was very early (6 weeks) and there was no medical opinion put forward to suggest that the accident caused the miscarriage or that the accident was intentional. It further highlighted the fact that they had a very weak case, with little evidence to present.

The defense called state trooper David Dicks to testify about the event. After going to the hospital, Jason and Michelle had returned to the scene to check on their vehicle and talk to police. The accident report written by Dicks indicated that both Michelle and Jason had been wearing their seatbelts at the time of the accident. Jason went off the road to the right and over-corrected to the left and down the embankment. No further investigation was warranted.

***

The prosecution completely ignored the three neighborhood witnesses who'd reported seeing a light colored SUV the morning of November 3. The defense called two of the witnesses. Terry Tiller testified that the house was lit up and it caught her attention because normally she would not be able to see the house, being that it was such a dark road and the house sat pretty far back from the road. Most of the lights were on and the driveway pillar lights were on. The SUV was parked parallel to the home, either in the street or in the driveway. She also described seeing a mini-van on the opposite side of the street. She testified that she would have been there between three-thirty and four o'clock, but in her initial police interview, she thought it was between four and five o'clock. This is important because if it was the latter, it couldn't have been Jason. He wouldn't have had enough time to get back to Virginia. During cross examination Tiller testified that she *could have* seen the SUV at the house as early as three o'clock that morning. That would fit the prosecution's timeline, but the earliest recollection of four to five o'clock is likely more accurate.

Cindy Beaver was also called by the defense to describe what she saw the morning of the murder. As stated previously, she described seeing a light colored SUV exiting the driveway with a male driver and female passenger. The driver was a thin, white male; the passenger had dark, bushy hair. She also noted there were lights on at the house, which was unusual for that time of the morning. She continued down Birchleaf and noticed a van on the right side street which was very close to the Young home. She described it as a delivery-type van, rather than a mini-van. She recalled that the interior lights were on and it appeared that the driver had papers spread out on the steering wheel. Cindy assumed it was a news delivery truck, but maybe it was someone connected to the crime.

During prosecution questioning Cindy described that there had been many visits from detectives and during the last interview the SBI agent had convinced her to state that she could not be certain she had seen the SUV on the day of the murder. Were police coercing her because the story didn't fit their theory? They had a witness who described seeing a woman matching Meredith Fisher's description, yet never pursued the possibility of her involvement.

***

Jason Testifies

Jason had to sit and listen to all the testimony about his potential motives for killing Michelle and all the various ways he "could have" accomplished it. After years of silence and the resulting isolation, Jason would finally have a chance to discuss *everything* — his relationship with Michelle and her family, his affairs, his past relationships, what he did the night of November 2nd, and how he'd coped with the civil lawsuits. It is the opinion of this author that his attorney was wrong to advise him to remain silent and basically cut himself off from everyone in his life. Jason surely needed to talk about everything. Family and friends would have been able to support him as he expressed his feelings about everything he'd experienced with the loss of his wife and unborn child. How painful must it have been for him to keep everything inside? Nonetheless, he trusted his attorney and believed it would all go away when the investigation failed to uncover evidence of his involvement. Little did he know how severely the government would use his silence against him.

Jason's testimony was solid and likely appealed to the jury. He was articulate, sensitive, and open. Prosecutor Becky Holt was unable to rattle him. Jason didn't stumble on any questions he was asked, even when they didn't paint him in the best light. He readily accepted responsibility for his failures. He seemed to be telling the truth.

Jason admitted to the challenges in his marriage. He described how he and Michelle had intimacy issues and how Linda was a source of conflict. He stated that it was true that he didn't want his mother-in-law to move into their home and that her extended visits were putting a strain on his marriage. It was making him unhappy, but Michelle didn't seem to understand that. He hated that Michelle would run to Linda when they argued because he knew it would make Linda like him less and he felt it was unfair. They had problems, but don't most married couples? Did it mean he wanted his wife dead? There was no indication of that.

Jason got choked up a few times, and it did not appear that he was faking it. He began to sob as he described how he'd learned of Michelle's pregnancy, how Cassidy was wearing the "big sister" t-shirt. He talked about shopping for baby clothes when they learned it was a boy and how they'd avoided choosing items of the standard baby blue color because it reminded them of *Carolina* blue (UNC colors). Both of them were huge NC State fans and the schools were fierce rivals. Jason loved being a father and couldn't wait to have a son, despite the conflict in the marriage. Michelle had been emotional lately, but she was the same way during her pregnancy with Cassidy, and Jason hoped she would return to her normal self after the baby was born.

Jason also sobbed when he was asked to describe the viewing at Michelle's funeral. He talked about the object he'd placed under Michelle's hand, such a personal and private moment as he said goodbye to his dear wife, yet it was important for the jurors to understand what he was experiencing. Jason would sometimes sing a song to Michelle that he'd known since childhood, "I love you, a bushel and a peck..." At one point, Michelle wrote down the lines from the song and slipped the paper into his wallet as a surprise. It was a cherished memory and Jason placed the memento under her hand so it would always be with her.

Jason's attorney continued to ask him questions, giving him an opportunity to explain everything put forward by the prosecution. There had been internet searches found on his computer with the terms "anatomy of a knockout" and "head trauma." Jason described how he'd witnessed a bad car accident and stopped to aid the victim of the crash. He found a man in the driver's seat with his head slumped on the steering wheel. He was bleeding and Jason was clearly shaken from the situation. He called for assistance but he described that he'd felt helpless as he waited for the paramedics to arrive. All he could do was hold the man's hand and talk to him as he tried to keep him calm and assure him that he wasn't alone. Jason got choked up as he explained that he didn't even know if he could hear him. The man was breathing when he'd first arrived, but shortly after paramedics administered treatment, they'd lost his pulse and then rushed him to the hospital. Jason did the internet searches because he wanted to know if there was anything else he could have done to help the man. The story was verified by an email that Michelle had sent to Shelly Schaad. Shelly worked as a nurse at the hospital and Michelle wanted to know if she was aware of a car accident victim who'd been treated that day because Jason was still shook up about it.

June 21 2006 Email from Michelle to Shelly:

Michelle: Were you able to find out anything about that guy who was in the accident? Jase was v. upset about it.

Shelly: The only thing I heard was about a guy who had surgery on his leg . . . he had some orthopedic surgery. There were three to four car accidents that day that all came to the ER!

* Note that this email was not presented at trial. This author came across it while reviewing the case files.

Next, Jason had an opportunity to discuss his relationship with Molly. He admitted that it was a mistake and that they both knew it could never go anywhere, yet they grew close as they both discussed the problems in their marriages.

Jason discussed the incident with Genny and the engagement ring. He admitted that he did pin her down and remove the ring, but that the rest of her claim was false. He didn't do anything that would have caused bruising. He admitted that he never should have touched her and that nothing like that had ever happened again. It's true that Jason was not known as a violent person. Not a single witness described him that way, but when one is accused of a crime, every intimate detail about their past becomes exposed making their entire life an open book. Thus the argument with Genny that got out of control became public knowledge used to imply that he was capable of harming his wife. Again, Jason's explanation was believable. His remorse over the situation seemed credible.

***

Everyone was anxious to hear from Jason about the night of November 2. What did he do after he'd checked into the Hampton Inn just minutes before 11 p.m.? It was actually quite uneventful. He went to his room and called Michelle to let her know he'd made it safely. He spoke to his friend Demetrius Barrett for a few minutes. He wanted to know more about a home warranty program that Demetrius' mother had purchased for her home. Jason was trying to figure out a way to pay for the repair of the upstairs heat pump with winter coming. Demetrius testified that the conversation was normal. Jason did not sound strange.

Jason had to explain why he was seen heading down the corridor leading to the exit door at two separate times. He said that the first time he left his room to get his computer charger from the car because he wanted to review some of the software for his presentation the following morning. Then he was seen at the front desk close to midnight. He said he'd stopped by to ask the clerk if he had a USA Today newspaper so he could take a look at the sports scores. He grabbed the newspaper and a bottled water and headed out the exit door a second time. He was not seen on camera again after that. He testified that he went out that same exit door to smoke a cigar and read the paper. After that he returned to his room, brushed his teeth and went to bed. There was computer activity up until midnight and he spoke to Molly before turning in.

The prosecution was unable to attack any of Jason's stories, aside from the cigar smoking. They drew attention to the fact that Jason hated smoking. He even made it a point to include a term in the custody agreement that Meredith could not smoke in the house with Cassidy living there. They wanted the jury to believe that he was making up the cigar smoking story because he actually left at that time to drive to Raleigh to commit the murder, but many cigar smokers despise cigarette smoke. They are two very different things.

ADA Becky Holt cross-examined Jason. There was not a single question about any evidence connecting him to the crime. One would expect a murder suspect to be asked about things that specifically tie them to the crime, but that was not so in this case. Holt spoke with a very loud voice throughout her questioning as she attempted to smear Jason. When one has evidence, there is no need to yell at the defendant. Holt first suggested that the Youngs had financial strain as she brought up Jason's online gambling habits. She suggested that Michelle wanted to sell the townhouse, but Jason simply explained that it wasn't true . . . that the townhouse was actually a very good investment for them.

Holt's questions focused on Jason's reaction to Linda's involvement in their lives. She pointed out that he didn't want her to move in, and that he didn't want her to go to Brevard with them for Thanksgiving, despite Michelle's wishes. She attempted to make him seem like an awful person, but perhaps many people feel the same way. How many people would actually want an overbearing mother-in-law to move into their home?

Holt went after Jason about trivial things as she asked him why he left the house "so late" when he had an appointment a great distance away the next morning. He had left the house at seven o'clock . . . how was that suspicious? Then she asked him why he parked his car on the side of the building at the Hampton Inn. Jason responded that it was the first available spot. Her questioning was ridiculous.

Holt's primary questioning centered on Young's failure to speak to the authorities. She pointed out that he'd chosen not to speak to police on November 3, but Jason explained that he wanted to wait until he spoke to an attorney. That was certainly reasonable. She made it clear that ignoring the custody suit meant he wouldn't have to sit for a deposition, but Jason said that he didn't have the money to respond to the suit—another reasonable explanation. How can one respond to a very costly civil suit when one can't even maintain a job? Jason spoke of the internet vigilante group that cost him every job he'd had since Michelle's death. His testimony made it clear that there was nothing he could do to maintain primary custody of Cassidy. He had been pushed into a corner.

It used to be the case that defendants were routinely encouraged to refrain from testifying because they'd be subjecting themselves to a brutal cross-examination, but in this particular case, it benefited Jason Young because he handled it very well. He *sounded* innocent.

***

The "absence of evidence" phrase that Klinkosum brought up in opening arguments came up again during closing arguments—this time by the prosecution. David Saacks stated, "No hotel fibers, right? It's supposed to mean he couldn't have done this. There's a common saying in the forensic world that says 'Absence of evidence is not evidence of absence.' Forensic evidence is a positive science, not a negative science." Saacks went on to cite an example that just because fingerprints are not found, does not mean the person wasn't present at the location. That's true, but the state must meet the burden of proof. We shouldn't consider that a person "may have" been somewhere when there is no evidence placing them there, especially when the person is facing life in prison. This is not the last time we would hear about the absence of evidence in this case.

Following closing arguments on Thursday June 23, 2011, the jury was given the case. They deliberated for a couple of hours that afternoon, and then all day Friday. After the weekend, they deliberated for two additional hours on Monday before sending a note to the judge stating "Unfortunately at this time we are at an impasse. We currently sit at a 6-6 ratio and do not appear to be able to make any further movement. Where do we go from here?"

Judge Stephens called the jury into the courtroom and instructed them to go back to the jury room to continue trying to reach a unanimous verdict. However, after a few more hours deliberating, the jury informed the court that they were immovably hung at 8 innocent, 4 guilty. Judge Stephens had no choice but to declare a mistrial.

CHAPTER 16

Jason is released

On July 20, 2011 the state announced its decision to retry Jason. This was a quick announcement in light of the fact that the majority of the jurors voted "not guilty." Why would twelve different people return a different verdict with the same evidence? Should the state even be permitted to try people over and over until they achieve a guilty verdict? Nonetheless they were moving forward with a new trial scheduled in October.

A week after the retrial announcement, Jason was released from the Wake County detention center on a $900,000 bond, secured with his mom's property.

His mother and step-father picked him up and took him to his sister Kim's home in Aberdeen. By that point he had been in jail for over eighteen months. Kim remembers they had a lot of his favorite foods for him. Everyone was relieved that they were able to get him released between the trials. Jason was overwhelmed after everything he'd been through and he knew it wasn't over.

Supervised visits with Cassidy were arranged at Time Together. Jason wanted to see Cassidy every week, but Meredith only agreed to twice a month visits. It was better than nothing though and at least he was free so that he could spend time with her. He had missed her so much while he was in custody awaiting trial.

The trial was pushed back a few months and would not begin until February, 2012. Jason spent that time hanging out in Brevard with family and would meet with his attorneys regularly to discuss the defense strategy. Although he was not looking forward to enduring another trial, he hoped to be acquitted this time.

CHAPTER 17

A new suspect?

During the trial, a woman by the name of Billie Hamilton contacted police and informed them that her grandson, Benjamin Hamilton may have been involved in Michelle Young's murder. Months later, another witness contacted the District Attorney's office with information about Hamilton and the Young case. Tony Gupton worked with local news station, WRAL and had information to share. At Detective Spivey's request, Gupton was interviewed by Officer Jebediah Yoakum at the Wake County Sheriff's Office in September, 2011. Gupton stated that between four and six weeks prior to the interview, he was at the Hamilton Machine Shop. He had been going there for several years to get his camera repaired and had become friendly with the Hamilton family. On this particular day he was making small talk with eighty year old Billie Hamilton. When Benjamin's name came up, she blurted out, "I know Ben killed that Young girl!" She further stated that Ben had come into a lot of money right after the murder. She described how Ben had "roid rage" and anger issues caused by years of steroid and drug use.

After listening to the trial testimony, it was Billie's belief that Jason Young had paid Ben to kill Michelle. She didn't have any knowledge that the two knew each other, but she had suspected Ben's involvement in the murder since just weeks after the murder and since it was known that Jason was in Virginia, she surmised that he may have paid her grandson to commit the murder. Had she been withholding this information all this time?

Detective Spivey interviewed Billie a few days prior to Gupton's interview. It is unclear why he didn't interview her at the sheriff's office or feel a need to interview her alone. The interview was conducted in her home in the presence of her husband, Robert. This was a person with possible information related to a homicide . . . information that would have been withheld for five years, yet they simply went to the woman's home to casually question her about her possible knowledge of the crime?

Billie informed Detective Spivey that Benjamin was at her house a couple weeks after the murder and that she had a newspaper lying on the table. The paper was opened to a story about the Young murder. According to Billie, Benjamin said "I bet he got someone to do it for him." Billie stated that this was the only conversation she had ever had with Benjamin about this matter and that it was untrue that he had come into money around that time period. Billie further stated that she had no reason to believe that Benjamin had anything to do with the murder, though she admitted that she did contact police during the trial to share the comment Benjamin had made. She also said that she spoke with Captain Ricky Martin with the Wake County Sheriff's Office about her suspicions about Benjamin and the Young case. She said she talked to him because he was familiar with all of Benjamin's troubles with the law the family had dealt with over the years. It is unclear at what time she had informed Captain Martin of this and Detective Spivey never asked that question.

Billie's denial that Benjamin had come into money after the murder is certainly inconsistent with Gupton's statement. What reason would he have had to lie? Did Billie hold back because her husband was present during the interview? It's certainly possible. She was concerned enough to call police and concerned enough to discuss this with Gupton, yet suspiciously after speaking to the lead detective of the Young murder—one who had completely overlooked this person as a suspect—she backtracked about her suspicions and about the money Benjamin had acquired near the time of the murder. Again, police should have questioned her at the police station alone and she also should have been questioned by an objective detective, one who was not involved in the Young investigation.

***

Benjamin Hamilton would have been twenty-five years old at the time of Michelle Young's murder. He grew up in Raleigh with his parents, Linwood and Rhonda Hamilton and his brother, Linwood Jr. He attended Wake Christian Academy and appeared to have had a stable childhood. He did well academically and excelled at sports, but problems began to surface beginning his junior year of high school. He had developed Lyme disease and was homeschooled that year but returned to Wake Christian his senior year. Something wasn't right with him though and police reports indicate that he began hanging out with a bad crowd and got involved in drugs. He lost interest in sports and his personality changed. Things really went downhill for him.

Benjamin became increasingly violent, likely due to his use of steroids and other drugs. He started becoming hostile toward his parents. They were afraid of him. He would storm into their home, throw things around in a rage and threaten to harm and even kill his parents. They had to call police on several occasions.

Benjamin had relationship problems as well. He was arrested for assault on a female when his girlfriend attempted to end their relationship. He became angry and refused to leave her home and would not allow her to leave. He threw her on the bed where she bumped her head on a side table and then went into the bathroom and began breaking things and throwing things. His girlfriend finally convinced him to leave and she quickly called the police. They suggested she take out a restraining order and she took that advice, but it didn't work. He continued to call her, to stalk her to follow her around and even began contacting neighbors and family. He wouldn't leave her alone. He was finally arrested for violating the order.

There were other incidents. At one point he broke into his parent's business and stole the keys to a work truck and then took the truck. His father contacted police and Benjamin was arrested and spent twenty-one days in jail. He threatened his father after that. Things were spiraling out of control. Years prior, in 2005 a friend of Benjamin's — John Pollard, was beaten so severely that he almost died.

Police in Chapel Hill questioned Benjamin in connection to the assault but he passed a polygraph and was thus never charged; however when Benjamin would attack his father, he made threats that he would do the same thing to him that he did to Pollard. Benjamin was a big man—220 pounds and very muscular and his father was very afraid of him. He was increasingly unstable and would be nice one day and become mean in an instant and become very destructive.

When Benjamin was released from jail, he needed a place to stay, so his parents felt they had no choice but to take him in. That was probably a mistake. Things weren't good. He continued to threaten them and even told them he wanted to kill his ex-girlfriend. Linwood contacted the girl to warn her.

Linwood and Rhonda were tired of living in fear of their own son. One night he was like a wild animal. Linwood ended up sleeping with a shotgun next to him. In the morning he started up with them again and Linwood insisted he had to leave, but he refused. He got physical with Linwood and kicked him when he was helping Benjamin toward the door. Linwood retreated to his bedroom. He and Rhonda were very afraid. Linwood told Rhonda to go into the bathroom. Linwood grabbed the shotgun and when Benjamin came storming down the hall toward them, he shot him in the chest. The shot was fatal. The tragic event occurred on June 27, 2010. After an investigation, the district attorney decided not to charge Linwood for the shooting due to the violence exhibited by Benjamin over the past several years.

***

Interviews with those close to the family were conducted as part of the investigation into the fatal shooting of Benjamin Harrison. Billie Harrison, along with her husband, Robert was interviewed at that time and she had a great deal of information to share about her grandson; contrary to her interview in the Young murder investigation.

> I asked Mr. and Mrs. Hamilton to describe Benjamin Hamilton, which Mrs. Hamilton described him as being angry and hateful. Mr. Hamilton described his grandson as he could be sweet but then turn around and cut your throat.

> Mrs. Hamilton stated they took Benjamin into their home shortly after high school to get him away from Linwood Hamilton Sr. Mrs. Hamilton stated they had to move Benjamin out of their house, and set up a bed in the shop for him. Benjamin became angry and damaged their shop. <u>Benjamin used paint to write satanic writings on the walls</u> of their shop. [xv]

Clearly he was a very disturbed individual, but the reference to satanic writings stood out to this author. There was more.

> Mrs. Hamilton stated her grandson had flexed his arms, showing her how large his bicep muscles were. As he was doing this he stated, "<u>I can hit and</u>

> kill anyone I want to; the law can't touch me and none of you could touch me."

Hamilton wasn't afraid to verbalize his belief that he could kill anyone he wanted and get away with it. Then there was another reference to Hamilton's interest in Satanism.

> Mrs. Hamilton stated they had previously had Benjamin's car towed to their shop, and they had found a satanic book in his car.

The reason Hamilton's interest in Satanism could be relevant is the fact that some experts describe overkill as a sign that the murder may have been an occult killing. Dawn Pelmutter, an expert on ritual killings and former director of the Institute for the Research of Organized and Ritual Violence describes such "overkill."

> Dawn Perlmutter: What distinguishes a ritualistic killing from a standard homicide is that it goes beyond what's necessary just to kill someone. There's overkill or mutilation. But even more than that, it's usually some kind of symbolic evidence. For example, symbols carved into the body, there can be symbols painted on the floor, it can be the positioning of the body, the staging. These are your pretty standard signs. They tend to be multiple homicides also. And then you get into other types of things, like significance of dates, or significance of holidays specific to different ideologies....[xvi]

While this may not have been an occult killing, there certainly was overkill—Michelle sustained at least thirty blows. Hamilton's possible involvement in the murder can't be easily dismissed. He was living with his parents in the Young's neighborhood of Enchanted Oaks at the time of the murder and was violent, unstable and abusing drugs. He also made statements about the murder to his grandmother that concerned her enough that she told a police officer about them, and then called the DA's office during Jason's trial. She also told a witness that Benjamin came into a large sum of money around that time.

Then there's Cassidy's description of a Mulan. Hamilton wore his hair in a pony-tail. Could that mean that she saw *him*?

Benjamin Hamilton

There are definitely indications that the killer(s) may have been under the influence of drugs and/or alcohol—all of the lights in the home were on, the killers were seen pulling out of the driveway early that morning, footprints were left, closets were rummaged through, jewelry was taken. The overkill manner of death could be consistent with a "roid rage" episode or an occult killing or drug induced mania. The state asserts that it was indicative of a personal crime, but maybe they were wrong. Hamilton certainly seemed like a strong suspect, but the investigation was limited since he was deceased and all of his belongings were gone.

Police and prosecutors were very invested in Jason Young at the time. They had already tried him once and were gearing up to prosecute the case again. This new suspect was likely an inconvenience. They were unable to connect Benjamin Hamilton to Jason Young, but should police have been trying to link him to someone else? Should they have attempted to link him to the bushy-haired woman (Meredith?) observed by Cindy Beaver? Was Hamilton the driver? Did they know each other? Hamilton worked at Ruth's Chris Steakhouse in 2006. Meredith worked at a different restaurant in the same town at that time. Is it possible that restaurant workers got together at the Ale House after work? There is no indication that there was any attempt to explore that possibility, but then Meredith was never considered a suspect.

Detective Spivey interviewed Linwood and Rhonda Hamilton after they'd received the tip from Gupton. Again, it would have been proper to interview them separately but police did not do so. The Hamiltons were adamant that Benjamin did not know Jason Young and they couldn't understand why Billie would have suggested he'd been involved in Michelle's murder. They did not recall that he'd come into money at the time. They informed police that their son wore size 12 Dingo boots around the time of the murder. All of his belongings had been disposed of, including his car.

Police had Harrison's DNA profile on file due to his prior arrests. It was compared to the unidentified DNA from the jewelry box and other items, but no match was found. That doesn't mean he wasn't involved—absence of evidence isn't evidence of absence! However, the investigation into his possible involvement ended there. There would be no mention of him at the new trial and the public never heard a word about this possible suspect.

CHAPTER 18

Trial two

Opening statements for the re-trial commenced on February 6, 2012. The prosecution would need a new strategy. They were unable to convince twelve people that Jason was guilty. What would they do differently? For starters, they changed up their team. David Saacks would be replaced by Howard Cummings. Cummings is the First Assistant District Attorney, one step below the district attorney. He had won a conviction in the Nancy Cooper murder case the prior year, a trial that would be one of the longest in Wake County's history. It lasted ten long weeks and was drawn out by Cummings' tendency to drone on and on with pointless questioning, boring the jurors, making them impatient for the trial to end. Jurors even sent a note to the judge stating that they wanted their lives back. Of course it was the judge who allowed the endless, insignificant questioning, but it seems very possible that dragging things out is part of his strategy. Cummings is also condescending, disrespectful and almost hostile toward defense witnesses in this author's opinion. It is offensive and difficult to listen to him bully witnesses in this manner, but he gets away with it. Becky Holt remained the second prosecutor.

Aside from a new prosecutor, in a desperate move, the state would also attempt to present *inadmissible* evidence this time around. Would the judge allow it? Judge Donald Stephens presided over Jason's first trial and he would remain in place for the re-trial. This is significant due to the nature of the evidence the state sought to present. They wanted the jury to hear about the civil lawsuits. This type of information is generally inadmissible because it is clearly prejudicial for a jury to hear that the accused had a civil judgment against them, and particularly in this case where there was a judgment declaring Jason the <u>slayer</u> (killer). The level of prejudice is magnified in this case because Judge Stephens signed the judgment against Jason, rather than delaying the judgment pending the outcome of the criminal case. It was certainly an option for him and would have made sense, but he chose to sign the judgment, making the case that much easier for the state to win due to the public's awareness of that action.

Aside from the inadmissible testimony about the wrongful death suit, the prosecution also wished to present hearsay evidence. They wanted Cassidy Young's daycare teachers to testify about observations they'd made while she played with dolls just days after the murder. This would come in under an "excited utterance" hearsay exception. This would also typically be considered inadmissible because the child was only two and a half at the time, and the observation had been made a week following the murder.

Becky Holt's opening arguments were very similar to those from the first trial, with the exception being the references to the civil law suits. She ended her arguments by informing the jurors that Jason remained silent instead of responding to the civil lawsuits. "Rather than answer questions, he gave up his daughter!" said Holt with an outraged tone of voice. She also brought up the wrongful death suit. "You will learn that there was a wrongful death suit filed with the allegation that the defendant murdered Michelle Young, and you will learn that instead of responding to that allegation the defendant defaulted because that would have meant he would have had to be subjected to a deposition. Instead of responding, he allowed a civil judgment to be entered against him!" Frankly, it does sound bad. How could he not fight for his daughter? How could he ignore a claim that he'd murdered Michelle? Why would an innocent person do such a thing? People don't realize that the way these civil suits went down, there was no possible positive outcome for Jason. As mentioned previously, the police detective filed an affidavit stating that he believed Jason was guilty of the murder. The District Attorney's office provided both of Linda Fisher's attorneys' full access to the investigative files. Jason would have spent hundreds of thousands of dollars (assuming he had it to spend, which he did not) and lost. Holt provided no mention of any physical evidence linking Jason to the murder.

    Much like the first trial, Jason's attorney, Mike Klinkosum focused on the fact that all the physical evidence pointed away from Jason and that the state's timeline didn't work. He stated that Jason did not kill Michelle and the crime has not been solved.

***

All of the trial testimony was longer. The second trial was almost twice as long as the first one. Gracie Bailey was spruced up this time with a new hair-cut, highlights and a suit. She looked like a completely different person. The prosecution spent a lot more time with her—showing diagrams of the store and asking her to describe her encounter with Jason in the early morning hours of November 3, but the defense readily refuted her testimony. They had obtained additional information about Gracie between the trials. She'd been hit by a car as a child and when questioned about it she described how her brain was lying on the pavement. She was lucky to have survived, but the injury left her disabled. She received disability payments for years. It explains why she was unable to describe what Jason looked like. Gracie was not a strong witness. The state needed more if they were going to convince twelve people that Jason was responsible for Michelle's death.

Moving on to the excited utterance hearsay testimony, Judge Stephens ruled to allow it. He believed the probative value outweighed the prejudice it would cause. He gave the jurors a limiting instruction citing that the jurors were to make no assumptions about the identity of the person(s) represented in the doll play. The prosecution proceeded and the testimony was almost funny if it weren't for the fact that someone's entire future was on the line.

ADA Cummings took all of the plastic toys up to the stand while Cassidy's daycare teacher, Ashley Palmatier testified about her observations. She described how she was walking around, checking on the children and noticed Cassidy was holding a "mommy" doll in one hand, and her other hand held an elderly lady doll with white hair, dressed in a purple jogging suit and holding a pink chair. The mommy doll had her hair in a brown pony tail, similar to how Michelle often wore hers. Palmatier said Cassidy took the chair and elderly doll and "hit" the mommy doll. When Palmatier asked Cassidy what she was doing, she said "Mommy's getting a spanking for biting. Mommy has boo-boos all over." Palmatier said Cassidy then laid the mommy doll face down on the plastic bed.

Following Cassidy's nap, she said. "Mommy was on the bed with boo-boos all over. Animals were in the barn. They were hungry. Daddy bought me fruit snacks." The judge felt the child's statements were too scattered to have any relevance, so the jury didn't hear the post-nap utterances. Maybe it would have been fairer for them to hear *all* of it to understand Cassidy's mindset.

Palmatier explained that there were approximately ten dolls in the bucket, including a male doll dressed in scrubs, yet Cassidy chose the female old lady doll. The prosecution introduced this testimony because they wanted to convince the jury that Cassidy had witnessed the murder. In doing so, it meant that the killer saw her and chose not to harm her. They wanted the jury to believe that the killer had to be Jason. Based on how calm Cassidy was when she was found, it seems unlikely she had witnessed the murder. As well, Cassidy showed no fear of Jason when he arrived in town that Friday evening. However, the jury was nonetheless left with the idea that Cassidy may have seen the murder.

Coincidentally, officer Karen Battle with the WCSO happened to be at the daycare center that very day to interview all of the workers who had ever interacted with Cassidy. It is unclear how police came up with the idea to interview the workers, or who sent Battle to the center. Palmatier seemed to indicate that she had contacted police after making the observations, but Battle testified for the state and was not asked a single question about her interviews with the daycare workers. It was very odd. That Thursday was also Cassidy's last day there, as Heather and Joe took her to their home to shield her from the media and family stress and drama. One may wonder why police made no effort to arrange for a child psychologist to speak to Cassidy in those early days following the murder, especially after learning about the doll play. Cassidy was certainly verbal enough to talk relay her thoughts. The prosecution wants people to believe that Jason committed the murder and that Cassidy was in the blood and cleaned up by Jason;

yet this child made no mention that her father was there. Did they refrain from having a child psychologist speak to Cassidy because they were worried her answers would not fit their theory?

***

In the first trial, the state didn't call any of the three witnesses who'd reported seeing the light colored SUV at the Young home the morning of November 3. This time they called the newspaper delivery woman. She had testified during the first trial that she *could have been* by the Young home as early as 3-3:30 that morning. Since that fit their timeline, she became a state witness for this trial. The suggestion was that Tiller saw Jason's Explorer that morning. It is interesting how this timeline shifted, as Tiller initially told police that she saw the SUV between four and five o'clock that morning. Naturally the earlier statement should have held more weight, but the state was desperately trying to make the evidence fit.

The state did not call the other two witnesses to testify because they reported seeing the SUV much later that morning. They opted to ignore them, since it didn't fit their timeline and it pointed away from Jason. Of course the defense called Cindy Beaver and Faye Hensley during their case in chief as they had in the first trial. This time the state attempted to discredit Beaver by calling her boss as a rebuttal witness. The prosecution elicited testimony from her boss, Jimmy Arrington who testified that Cindy Beaver was a "busybody," implying that she'd provided the information to police for attention. So the witness made up a story for attention and it coincidentally included a sighting of a light SUV that the other two witnesses had observed. It was offensive that they would treat a witness that way, but more so, this claim didn't make a bit of sense. Beaver wasn't even going to call police to report what she'd seen. It was Arrington who'd contacted them on her behalf because he believed it could be important to the investigation. This pathetic attempt to discredit a witness further illustrated how weak the state's case was.

The prosecution called Fiona Childs to testify about the Youngs' estate planning. In July 2005, Michelle sought Fiona's assistance in drafting a will for her and Jason. At that time Cassidy was over a year old and they felt it was important to designate guardians to ensure she would be properly cared for if anything should happen to them. According to Fiona, the Youngs considered Meredith, but they felt it best to designate Heather and Joe for stability reasons. They were a married couple and hoped for children of their own. They would be better prepared to care for Cassidy than Meredith who worked a waitress job and attended school. However, they did have Fiona include a clause that the guardianship would be reconsidered in three years.

In addition to the wills, Michelle also asked Fiona about life insurance. Fiona couldn't help them with that, but she told Michelle that it was a smart idea, especially when there were children in the marriage. Michelle and Jason ended up getting large policies on each other in the amount of two million dollars. Michelle explained to Fiona that Jason wanted to ensure that Cassidy would be cared for. He had lost his father at a young age and naturally there were some financial struggles with the loss of that income. He didn't want Cassidy to experience anything like that. Michelle arranged for the policies for her and Jason because she was a C.P.A and was able to get a discounted rate. There was also a double indemnity clause for accidental death. That is why the plan paid four million dollars for Michelle's death. Apparently murder is included in the AD&D clause. The prosecution elicited the testimony as an indication that the insurance was motive for murder, but they failed to do so, as it was Michelle who had insisted on obtaining the policies and she who purchased them after they had agreed as a couple on the amount of coverage. Perhaps if the Youngs had been experiencing financial problems, money could have been a motive, but they were not. Both had good jobs with good salaries and no problems paying the bills.

***

The state's final witness was Wake County Clerk of Court, Lorrin Freeman. She was called to testify about the wrongful death suit—the timing, the terms and the outcome. Before getting into that, Howard Cummings questioned her about Jason's bond. Remember that his mother used her property as collateral to get Jason freed on bond between trials. The value of the land was sufficient to meet the nine-hundred thousand dollar bond. The prosecution wanted to show the jury that Jason had access to funds via his family which would have afforded him representation. Howard Cummings later questioned Pat Young about the value of her land, hoping the jury would wonder why she didn't sell it so that Jason could afford to respond to the suits. The money would have been thrown away because he most certainly would have lost with the lead investigator's affidavit stating that he believed Jason killed Michelle. How does one overcome something like that?

Before Freeman testified about the wrongful death suit, Judge Stephens asked the defense if they had any objections to the forthcoming testimony. They objected to the entire line of questioning based on rule 403 which basically states that the testimony would create undue prejudice and should be excluded, but the Judge overruled the objection. This meant that the jury would hear that Judge Stephens himself entered a default judgment declaring Jason the slayer.

Judge Stephens instructed the jury that a civil judgment was not a determination of guilt, but would that instruction be enough to overcome the prejudice from Freeman's testimony? Jason's attorneys could have objected based on another statute—rule 1-149 and that would have preserved the objection for appeal purposes, but they failed to do so.

The inclusion of the civil case testimony set a precedent. It is unusual in the first place for a wrongful death suit to precede a criminal case, but on the rare occasion when it has occurred, the civil judgments have only been allowed to be included under very special circumstances. One circumstance is impeachment. If the defendant's testimony during a civil proceeding is inconsistent with that of the criminal proceeding, the state may be permitted to use that for impeachment purposes. That certainly didn't apply to this case, since Jason didn't respond to the civil case.

What reason did the state have for introducing the civil testimony in this trial? They wanted to say "What?! That was all he had to say? He testified during his first trial about his reasons for leaving the hotel room to smoke a cigar and retrieve his computer cable. If that was all he had to say, why did he remain silent for year?" It wasn't impeachment, it was their weak attempt to discredit his statements, or at least that's the reason they would later offer. The truth is they used it to damage Jason. They found a way to get inadmissible evidence before the jury.

On March 6, 2012 after ten hours of deliberations, the jury found Jason *guilty* of first degree murder. Jason was sentenced to life in prison. Oral notice of appeal was given.

Following the verdict, some of the jurors spoke about how they'd arrived at the verdict. The news headline read "Lacking physical evidence pointed to Jason Young's guilt." Lacking physical evidence . . . *absence of evidence* . . . what were the jurors referring to? Believe it or not, it came down to the missing shoes and shirt. The jurors expected Jason to produce those items to prove his innocence. Was that proper, or did the jurors have things backward? First consider the hushpuppy shoes. They were purchased seven years before the trial. How many people remember what they did with a particular pair of shoes from several years ago? Recall that the shoes were purchased in the summer of 2005. When Jason testified at the first trial, he said that he believed Michelle likely donated the shoes to Goodwill. The pair of Kenneth Cole shoes found in the cargo area of the Explorer likely replaced that pair of shoes. They were the same style of shoes—brown, slip-on, casual shoes that Jason liked to wear with jeans. Isn't it a stretch to suggest that Jason switched shoes specifically to commit the murder? Is there evidence of that? No, there is not.

Regarding the shirt, we know that police didn't do a very good job inventorying the items from the Explorer. They didn't even take photos of each item. Some of the items obtained from the vehicle were not even listed on the evidence sheets. The state was required to prove guilt. Jason shouldn't have been expected to prove his innocence by producing these particular items.

The jury members also had an issue with the way Cassidy was found. Jury foreman, Tracey Raksnis stated that only Jason would have cleaned up Cassidy—certainly not a random burglar. During closing arguments the state made the case that it was most logical that Jason cleaned up Cassidy and that a stranger would never do something like that. That's true, but no consideration was given to Meredith having possibly cared for her.

Finally, the jurors had an issue with Jason's failure to testify. That is improper and in fact they were specifically told not to hold that against him. It is sometimes unsettling to hear the comments by jurors, especially when it is clear that they are not following instructions during deliberations. They seemed to expect Jason to prove his innocence in this case and that was improper.

There were two recent cases in which there were retrials ordered on appeal—the Russ Faria case and the Cal Harris case. Both men opted for a bench trial in which the judge alone would issue the verdict. It is commonly recommended to choose a jury trial, since twelve people are needed to vote guilty. Russ Faria was acquitted in his second trial. Cal Harris was acquitted in his *fourth* trial, having been found guilty by a "jury of his peers" at the three prior trials. So maybe juries are less objective these days than a judge; particularly when they are manipulated by unethical prosecutors willing to do anything to win a conviction.

As for the Young conviction, the defense probably did a more effective job at highlighting Meredith's inconsistencies and suspicious behaviors during the first trial. This jury didn't seem to catch on to the fact that she should have been investigated as a suspect and that she could have cleaned up Cassidy. Also, in this trial, the defense could have presented evidence about Benjamin Hamilton as a possible suspect, but for whatever reason they did not do so.

If one disregards the gas station clerk's testimony—she couldn't even accurately describe Jason; and disregards the camera tampering—the evidence didn't point to Jason, what's left . . . Jason's silence? Jason's infidelities? They didn't have much of a case.

What about Jason's silence? Was it proper for the state to use it against him? To begin, there is a difference between invoking ones right to remain silent outside of custody versus after an arrest. Make no mistake, silence *can* be used against you and it certainly was in this case. If Jason had been arrested in connection to this crime and at that point invoked his 5th amendment right, prosecutors wouldn't have been permitted to use that against him in court. This was different. They were allowed to point out his silence as suspicious before the arrest, both to police and his family and friends. For this reason, it was probably a mistake for Jason's attorney to have him refrain from all communication with investigators. Nonetheless, it was done and Jason was convicted. He was sent to the Alexander Correctional Institution in Taylorsville, North Carolina to begin serving his sentence. An appeal was filed shortly after his conviction, but the legal process moves slowly.

CHAPTER 19

Appeal

Jason's appeal was finally filed sixteen long months after the conviction. The process is slow. Transcripts need to be obtained, the appeal attorney needs to become familiar with the specifics of the case and then submit a brief. After that, the state is given time to respond and then finally oral arguments are scheduled. It's important to understand that the first appeal following a conviction is all about procedures—did the judge abuse his discretion to such a degree that it created an unfair trial? Also understand that once a person is convicted, the presumption of innocence is gone and it becomes a huge uphill battle. It is very difficult to get a conviction overturned. Approximately 1% of convictions are reversed based on judicial rulings.

Oral arguments were set for December 12, 2013. Jason was represented by Barbara Blackman. Without delving too deeply into the legal issues at hand, the appeal was largely based on the question of whether or not the judge should have allowed testimony about the civil suits.

Argument:

The trial court committed reversible error in admitting testimony relating to a wrongful death action and declaration under the slayer statute that Mr. Young killed his wife, Mr. Young's default, and entry of judgment.

No reference was made at the first trial to a wrongful death judgment and slayer determination obtained by Linda Fisher before Mr. Young's arrest. The trial ended in a hung jury. The State told the jury in opening statement on retrial that a wrongful death action was filed alleging that Mr. Young killed his wife, he defaulted, and judgment entered against him.

Before the State called the Clerk of Court to testify about the civil action, the defense objected, pursuant to Rule 403 "to the entire line of questioning about the wrongful death case." The court overruled the objection and ruled that the evidence was relevant and possessed probative value outweighing its prejudice.

The clerk's recitation of allegations in the pleadings and testimony that Mr. Young defaulted by failing to respond was inadmissible under NC statute 1-149 and <u>automatically</u> preserved for de novo review. [xvii]

> NC Statute 1-149:
> **No pleading can be used in a criminal prosecution against the party as proof of a fact admitted or alleged in it.**

There were other issues noted in the appeal, but this was the main focus of the oral arguments so the other issues will not be referenced at this time.

The state responded.

Argument:
The trial court did not abuse its discretion in admitting the civil default judgments.

Defendant testified at his first trial in June of 2011, providing his first ever account of his activities on 3 November 2006. His testimony was then in the second trial able to be rebutted and undermined in many new and particular ways. Among them, the State argued that defendant's statement that he was at the Hampton Inn in Virginia all night but that his key-card use would not reveal that because of the way he propped the doors to go outside to get something from his vehicle and smoke a cigar, was not credible in light of his lack of response to the wrongful death and insurance disqualification suits.

Defendant could have said everything he said in his testimony, if it were true, in response to the civil suits, and he had major incentives to do so; so he said nothing about his activities and purposefully avoided giving any deposition. Thus, the State used his reaction to the civil suits to show that he likely manufactured his later story to try to fit it to the evidence against him.

Defendant cited only Rule 403 when he objected to the introduction of the civil matters. He did not cite or obtain a ruling on either 1-149 or hearsay rules. 1-149 is not among the "mandatory duty" statutes that the courts have said preserve an issue for review without an objection.

(There was more, but this was the main argument)

The State justified the inclusion of the civil suits by asserting that Jason had everything to lose by remaining silent and that simply responding to the complaints would have assured that he would both maintain physical custody of his daughter and be able to collect the life insurance money. They wanted the jury to believe that silence meant guilt. Of course it was not quite that simple.

The State understood that they couldn't offer the civil suit testimony for the truth of the matter, so they *claimed* it was for impeachment purposes. How was the inclusion of the testimony really impeaching him though? The suggestion was that his testimony at the first trial impeached his *silence*. It didn't really make sense. How could statements be used to discredit silence? They hated that he'd remained silent until his first trial and they figured out a way to manipulate the system by claiming that the civil testimony was presented to impeach his very simple and straightforward statements. The judge allowed them to get away with it and it was very damaging testimony. The inclusion of the testimony surely influenced the jury. The first jury didn't hear any of it and they voted eight to four not guilty.

The prosecution crossed the line and got away with it. They did win their conviction. It was really unfair because it wasn't as simple as they made it out to be. This was described earlier, but remember that Jason was in a lose/lose scenario when Linda filed the suits against him because her attorneys were aligned with the prosecution. The prosecution gave them full access to the case files and the lead investigator filed affidavits for each lawsuit stating that he believed that Jason was guilty of murdering Michelle. It didn't matter that he had no evidence to support that belief. It sealed Jason's fate. There would be no possible way to win against the government.

Had it just been Linda versus Jason, things may have been different. The State had everything to gain by participating in the civil actions against Jason. It was a win/win for them—Force Jason to talk or alternatively force him to spend what little money he had left fighting the suits. He would have nothing left to defend against the impending criminal charge. Ultimately he would lose, whether he responded or not—and they knew it.

The prosecution also attempted to impeach Jason's statements about his financial position at the time the civil suits were filed against him. Jason testified that money was one of the reasons he didn't respond to the civil actions. They elicited testimony from Detective Spivey that Jason had 401K money and that he could have used that it to hire legal representation in the civil suits. That amount of money—approximately sixty-thousand dollars wouldn't have put a dent in the legal expenses required to respond to the suits.

ADA Howard Cummings then suggested that since Jason was out on bond, he could have used the bond money to respond to the suits. That wasn't true. His mother had put up her property to get him released on bond between trials. Was Cummings suggesting that she should have sold her property and home so that Jason could respond to the civil suits? Yes, he was. Again, it would have been impossible to win, even if Jason had a billion dollars in the bank, but it's unclear if the jury understood this. There should be a statute that bars police and prosecutors from assisting with civil suits when there is an active criminal investigation involving that person. This case set a precedent to use civil suits when there is insufficient evidence to arrest a person. It is a convenient way to force a suspect to submit to an interrogation (deposition) or use it against them if they decide to maintain their silence.

***

Jason won his appeal. The North Carolina Court of Appeals unanimously granted Jason a new trial on April 1, 2014, just over two years after his conviction. The process moves slowly, which can be especially difficult for the wrongly convicted and their families.

Decision:

The introduction into evidence of the civil complaints and judgment was in error and violated N.C. General Statute 1-149, as the evidence was used to prove a fact—namely, that Defendant had killed Michelle—Defendant is deemed to have admitted in the wrongful death civil action and which had been alleged in the child custody proceeding. This evidence also severely impacted Defendant's ability to receive a fair trial. As such, we order a new trial."[xviii]

The appeals court considered 1-149 a statutory mandate, which meant that an objection was not required. The court should have known not to allow the testimony. Unfortunately, the North Carolina Supreme Court disagreed and in August, 2015 they reversed the Court of Appeals decision. The case was sent back to the Superior Court so that Jason could pursue his other points of the appeal not previously argued before the appeals court.

The Supreme Court stated that 1-149 was not in fact a statutory mandate and that Jason's attorney needed to properly object to the civil suit testimony on that basis. For this reason, an ineffective assistance of counsel motion was also filed on Jason's behalf. As of August, 2016 Jason is still in prison waiting for the additional legal proceedings to play out. Until then, there is nothing he can do but wait. He can't have his case considered by an Innocence group until all appeals have been exhausted.

CHAPTER 20

Author's thoughts

I began researching the Young case shortly after Jason was convicted. Jason's sister, Kim reached out to me and I slowly began looking into the case and we eventually obtained the case files and were able to get a much clearer picture of how the investigation and prosecution were handled. I felt compelled to write this book to expose the unfairness of our justice system. This case is a good example to highlight that.

To begin, the introduction of the civil suits into the second trial was unacceptable. The prosecution and especially the judge had to know about the statute that barred the inclusion of the testimony. Basically, the State found a loophole to say "See, he was already declared the slayer in the civil case, so he must be guilty." Obviously it was prejudicial enough to affect the verdict. It's possible the US Supreme Court would disagree with the NC Supreme court over whether this was a statutory mandate or not, but nonetheless, Jason Young became a victim of this unfair legal maneuver.

The timing of the filings of the lawsuits against Jason was interesting. In the summer of 2008, there was another murder investigation underway in Wake County. Brad Cooper was the prime suspect in the murder of his wife, Nancy Cooper. Much like the Young case, there was no evidence linking him to her death. Both cases were very high profile and made national headlines. There was great pressure for police to solve them quickly.

Nancy's family filed for custody of the Cooper's two daughters, ages two and four shortly after she was found murdered. Just months later, a wrongful death suit was filed against Jason Young. Coincidentally, the law firm that represented Nancy's family—Tharrington-Smith also represented Jason Young, so they were involved in both law suits but represented the plaintiff in one and the defendant in another. In both cases the police and district attorney's office aligned with the plaintiffs, placing enormous pressures on Jason and Brad in cases that were now impossible to win. Both men would have their children taken from them and there was not a thing they could do.

Brad tried. He fought for his daughters at a custody trial. There was no testimony indicating that he was a bad father. He was a Cisco engineer with a stable job and was ambitious in his career. He had recently earned his MBA at NC State. He was very hands on with the children and often cared for them when his wife was out with friends. There was no domestic violence in the household. Brad had no criminal record. In fact, he didn't even have a speeding ticket. He and his parents spent an enormous amount of money fighting to keep the children. He submitted to a psychological examination and a seven hour deposition—exactly what Jason would have had to endure. Brad was indicted days after the custody trial. His efforts were all for naught. Nancy's sister was awarded custody of the girls. They were taken to Canada and are being raised there not knowing their father. Brad had no chance of winning because the government was aligned with the plaintiff's law firm, identical to Jason's situation.

It was unfair and unethical for the prosecution to portray Jason as a poor father in his failure to respond to suits that he could never win, but that is what they did. The prosecution chose to try the case knowing that there were major inconsistencies with Meredith Fisher's story and that she had an unverified alibi. Instead of acknowledging that three witnesses saw an SUV in the Young's driveway during a time that excluded Jason, they attempted to discredit the witnesses. They put a brain-damaged clerk on the stand to testify that she'd seen Jason that morning, knowing that she couldn't even describe what he looked like. They presented the fabricated camera tampering story, knowing that Jason's DNA and fingerprints were not found on the camera. Nothing linked him to Michelle's death, yet the prosecution's tactics resulted in his conviction. This is how wrongful convictions happen.

Despite numerous recent exonerations, there are still innocent people being railroaded into prison for crimes they didn't commit. The killers remain free. The public is duped, believing that there must have been enough evidence for the jury to find them guilty. Unless things change, it will continue to happen.

I believe that Jason will ultimately be exonerated. Even if this next round of appeals is unsuccessful, there is a lot of evidence in the case that can be reviewed. I found a lot of things that were not included in the trials that strengthen his case for innocence and will remain in contact with his attorneys until he is free.

***

Jason is surviving as best as possible while he waits for the justice system to process his remaining appeals. One thing that keeps him going is his knowledge that he is innocent. Since he is located near the mountains, his mom is able to visit him regularly. She also has periodic visits with Cassidy and is very grateful to still have her in her life while she waits and hopes to someday see her son freed.

Meredith purchased a new home and got married in 2015. Cassidy continues to reside with her but if Jason is exonerated, custody can always be revisited.

ABOUT THE AUTHOR

Lynne Blanchard resides in Raleigh, North Carolina with her husband and two sons. Her background is in polymer chemistry where she spent several years working in research and development, technical service and sales.

Lynne began researching cases with questionable verdicts in 2011 and has highlighted several cases on her blog. She published a book about Brad Cooper's wrongful conviction in 2015 after researching the case in great depth.

Lynne is currently doing paralegal work for The Deskovic Foundation for Justice.

Contact: lablanchard@nc.rr.com

twitter

Blogs:

Stop Wrongful Convictions

Justice for Jason Young

Justice for Brad Cooper

Framed: An Examination of the Nancy Cooper Murder Case was originally published in October, 2015 as *Framed With Google Maps*. The new edition released in September 2016 includes title and cover changes and minor changes with the interior text.

Can the government withhold evidence that could prove your innocence? In this shocking case, the state of North Carolina cited national security reasons for doing just that. It crippled any possible defense case for Brad Cooper who was charged with the murder of his wife, Nancy in 2008.

Nancy left home to go jogging and never returned. She was later found murdered. A shoddy and corrupt investigation followed, as evidence was destroyed and mishandled; witnesses were coached and evidence of innocence was ignored.

Learn the facts about this tragic case that will leave you appalled at the state of our justice system.

[i] Narrative #37

[ii] Deputy Earp's narrative #4

[iii] Deputy Tanner narrative #8

[iv] Photos courtesy of Dr. Maurice Godwin

[v] Meredith interview w/ Duane Deaver, SBI Sept 2007

[vi] Detective Sternberg narrative #365

[vii] Detective Ikerd narrative #425

[viii] Forensic Magazine June issue, p. 10-11

[ix] Duane Deaver's hand notes 7/21/07

[x] Search Warrant 2007

[xi] Narrative #66 interview with Det. Blackwell, Boyette

[xii] Linda Fisher interview with Det. Sternberg 3/1/07 narrative #361

[xiii] Spivey affidavit

[xiv] Judge Stephens judgment in claim Linda Fisher versus Jason Young

[xv] 7/21/10 interview with Detective Blomgren, narrative #30

[xvi]

[xvii] Jason Young's appeal 7-29-13

[xviii] NC Appeal decision 4-1-2014

Made in the USA
Middletown, DE
18 January 2017